An Exile of Ireland

James Campbell .

An Exile of Ireland

Hugh O Neill

Prince of Ulster

Micheline Kerney Walsh

FOUR COURTS PRESS

Published by
FOUR COURTS PRESS
Kill Lane, Blackrock, Co. Dublin, Ireland
and in North America by
FOUR COURTS PRESS
c/o ISBS, 5804 N.E. Hassalo Street, Portland, OR 97213.

The first edition of this book, along with original documents,
was published in 1986 by Cumann Seanchais Ard Mhacha.
This new edition was published in 1996

A catalogue record for this title
is available from the British Library.

ISBN 1-85182-234-8

Printed in Ireland
by Colour Books Ltd, Dublin.

Contents

I ndil chuimhe ar
an gCairdinéal Tomás Ó Fiaich
+ 1990

Foreword

When Hugh O Neill reached the outskirts of Rome with about thirty companions on 29 April 1608, he was met at the Ponte Milvio, the historic bridge over the Tiber to the north of the city, by Archbishop Peter Lombard, my twenty-fourth predecessor as Archbishop of Armagh. It was the place where Roman armies, returning in triumph along the Via Flaminia, had been welcomed home since the days of the Caesars. Emperor Maxentius was thrown into the Tiber at this spot following his defeat by Constantine in 312. To meet O Neill there the Archbishop had brought eight coaches, with six horses to each coach, and a number of smaller coaches, all provided by the Roman Cardinals for the occasion. Armagh, its Archbishop and the Sacred College of Cardinals were all brought together in this gesture of honour to 'The Great O'Neill'.

It is appropriate, therefore, that the present fine volume on O Neill's stay in Rome and the years immediately before should be published by the Armagh Diocesan Historical Society, Cumann Seanchais Ard Mhacha. O Neill was a native son of this archdiocese, born in Dungannon, brought up for some time in Dundalk, resident for much of his life in Dungannon Castle, proclaimed traitor in Dundalk by Queen Elizabeth and inaugurated as O Neill on the hill of Tullyhogue. The Yellow Ford, scene of his greatest military victory, was within the confines of the archdiocese of Armagh, as were the string of island fortifications which made him so hard to dislodge: Creeve, Roughan, Lough Rourkan, Marlacoo and Curran. So also were several of the castles and fortified posts erected for his overthrow: Moyry, Mountnorris, Mountjoy. He claimed the right of presentation to many of the parishes of this archdiocese and tried to have his own nominees appointed as Dean and Archbishop. When overthrown, he brought the sacred vessels of Armagh Cathedral for safe keeping to the Friars of Louvain. He commissioned Lombard in Rome to keep Ireland's case before the Papal Court. As Lombard's successor I am honoured to be invited by Cumann Seanchais Ard Mhacha to contribute a preface to this scholarly work.

I have always been intrigued by the character and personality of Hugh O Neill. More than any other Irishman of the 16th century he was an amalgam of Gaelic chieftain and Renaissance prince. His vision of politics, at first confined to the Mid-Ulster territory of his ancestors, was soon extended to include the whole of Ireland and ultimately embraced a keen awareness of its European dimension as well. Long before the

Confederation of Kilkenny began its hopeless task of uniting Gael and Anglo-Irish, he surrounded himself with a series of able executives from the two traditions, O Hagans and O Quinns, Dean Mac Donnell and his own brother Cormac from the former, Weston and Hovendon, Bath and Archer from the Old and New English. From a religious outlook which bordered on indifference he developed during his last decade in Ireland into an ardent figure of the Counter-Reformation. His Pale upbringing, his education in England, his marriage entanglements, his combination of attachment to traditional ways and preparedness to experiment in the organisation of Ulster, his durability as a 'survivor' in an era when so many of his contemporaries met death on the battlefield, by political assassination or by execution, his military prowess in defeating, defying or evading some of the greatest English commanders of the Elizabethan age, all these things gave him a complexity which has never been adequately explored. Seán Ó Faoláin in *The Great O'Neill* was the first to attempt it but, as the present documents were not available to him, his book ends for all practical purposes in 1602 and the final section '1602-1616: Exile and Epilogue' is less than worthy of the rest. Fortunately Micheline Kerney Walsh begins where Ó Faoláin ends and documents from the Spanish archives become more plentiful from 1605-6 on, when the plans for an escape from Ireland began to take shape.

O Neill's journey across half of Europe in 1607-8, accompanied by O Donnell, Maguire and their retinue, is one of the great epics of Irish history. Every schoolchild knows it as 'The Flight of the Earls', a phrase which deserves to be expunged from an Irishman's vocabulary after the publication of this book but which is unlikely to disappear. The book throws a flood of new light on the last fourteen years of O Neill's life, from the months of near despair in 1602 after the defeat at Kinsale to his lonely death in Rome in 1616.

From a series of more than two hundred and forty letters, reports and memorials written between those two dates, many of which have never previously been published, O Neill emerges with enhanced stature and more impressive gifts, a giant among his contemporaries and a leader whose place in our history has not yet been accurately appraised. Not only Ó Faoláin but earlier biographers of O Neill have been inclined to skim over these final years because of the dearth of source material in Irish and English archives. It is a pleasure therefore to welcome the 'release on the market' of this new Spanish material, copied over many years by Micheline Kerney Walsh and now presented in an English translation together with a detailed study by her of the last fourteen years of O Neill's life. I congratulate her warmly on the completion of what has been a most demanding task as well as a labour of love.

The story begins with the departure of Red Hugh O Donnell for Spain after Kinsale to seek further aid. O Neill was left to bring his troops back to the North, defeated, yet still strong and full of fight. But one after another of his allies began to seek separate peace terms and he was gradually hemmed around on all sides in the wooded territory of Glanconcadhain.

Just outside the village of Desertmartin in South Derry is Loch Lugg with the remains of a crannog. Here, according to tradition, O Neill and a handful of followers spent much of 1602. O Neill had a price on his head. A Spanish source states that £3,000 was offered for his capture if taken alive and £2,000 for his head if killed, the equivalent of more than £100,000 in present day values. Yet while his former allies were prepared to abandon him, none of them betrayed him. The news of Red Hugh's death in Spain on 10 September 1602 was a further blow to O Neill's hopes of further aid. Throughout that year Queen Elizabeth refused to permit any negotiations with him.

It is not surprising that as 1602 drew to a close O Neill saw little prospect of holding out much longer. The first O Neill letter in the present collection was written on Christmas Eve 1602 to King Philip III of Spain. It was a *cri de coeur* from a man that was nearing despair:

Most powerful king, it is impossible to describe to you the full extent of our misfortunes: we are awaiting the help of Almighty God and yours without delay. In your service we exhausted all our resources, suffered greatly and, half naked, have been brought by our enemies to the edge of destruction because of the promise which we gave you and which we have never yet broken . . . all the nobles who were with us previously have now left us and, having changed sides, have now become our enemies, so that the number of our followers is extremely reduced . . . Therefore in the name of God we beg Your Majesty to be moved by the miseries which we suffer and to send help to us . . . we pray Your Majesty to send us your help without delay; and should it not be your pleasure to send this help before the feast of St Philip and St James, we beg you to send a warship to the northern part of Ireland so that we may be conveyed to you, safe from the fury of our enemies.

This was O Neill's first intimation to Spain that if he received no further aid he would seek to go into exile. His letter did not reach Brussels until April 1603 and by that time he had accepted favourable terms from Mountjoy just before the death of Queen Elizabeth. King James received him in London during the summer and when peace between England and Spain was signed in August 1604, each promised not to support the rebellious subjects of the other. Thus deprived of Spanish backing O Neill soon found himself threatened by dangers on all sides – some of his lands claimed by others, his income reduced, attempts made to poison him or to bring him to imprisonment in London.

The factors which induced O Neill to leave Ireland in 1607 have always been a matter of controversy among historians. I was hoping that the present documents would solve many of the outstanding problems. What they do is confirm that Christopher St Lawrence's disclosures about a Catholic plot for an uprising had a basis in fact, though it was not as far advanced as he imagined. There was really a league of Irish Catholics in existence, including many from the cities and towns, who planned to seize a number of centres with aid from Spain, but they had not yet tried to contact the King there. The documents also confirm O Neill's view that if he had gone to London when invited in 1607 he would have been arrested

and possibly executed. Indeed he probably received information to this
effect from the Earl of Northampton, as six members of King James's
Privy Council, including Salisbury, Mountjoy and Northampton, were at
this time secretly in receipt of pensions from the King of Spain. Micheline
Kerney Walsh guides us adroitly through this maze of intrigue and
identifies the code-names by which some of the six were recognised in
diplomatic correspondence. She also succeeds in clearing up the confusion
which has hitherto existed concerning the name of the Captain who
brought the Earls to safety. He was Captain John *Rath,* not Bath.

In regard to the actual sea-voyage and the journey across Northern
France and Flanders, from Quillebeuf to Louvain, these documents add
nothing to Ó Cianáin's account. But from Louvain on they are of
immense value in bringing to light the secret intrigues which were going
on throughout the winter of 1607-8. The Archduke, under English
pressure, wished the Earls to leave Flanders and the Nuncio tried to
dissuade them from going to Rome and urged them to rely for help on the
King of Spain. They finally decided to go to the Spanish territory of
Milan, there to await the King of Spain's reply to the appeal they had sent
him from Louvain. For the Spaniards O Neill was now an embarrassment
as long as the peace with England lasted, but they could not afford to
alienate him completely as he would be very useful to them if the war were
resumed. The Spanish ambassador in London summed up the position
very accurately for King Philip in one of the documents published here:

. . . *the Earl of Tiron's departure from Flanders was not to his* [O Neill's]
pleasure and satisfaction; here [in London] *it has caused great rejoicing. I know
that they* [the English] *wish to kill him by poison or by any possible means . . .
It will be well that Your Majesty keep him well disposed to your royal service
for, to the English, he is a bridle. Their fear of him gnaws at their entrails and it
will be all the greater if he may go to Rome, for they believe that if Your Majesty
should send a hundred men with him to Ireland, all of that Kingdom would rise
against them.*

That letter indicates how the present volume complements Ó Cianáin
from the arrival of the Earls in Louvain until they reached Rome. The
documents published here are political and diplomatic, sometimes written
to deceive or hoodwink the recipient; Ó Cianáin, on the other hand, a
simple unsophisticated scribe, somewhat naive and medieval in outlook,
was obviously not *au fait* with the political chicanery which revolved
around his master's destination and wrote like an Irish country lad seeing
the Taj Mahal for the first time. We have to go to Ó Cianáin therefore for
the little personal touches on 'the path to Rome': the bad lodgings in La
Boissière; the terrible road from Wavre to Namur; the heavy snow and ice
in the St Gotthard Pass which compelled the travellers to use sleighs drawn
by oxen; the crossing of Lake Lucerne and Lake Lugano by boat; the tragic
accident on the Teufelsbrücke in the Alps when one of the horses fell into a
ravine below with the loss of £100 (the equivalent of several thousand
pounds today); the dinners with the Archdukes in Binche and with the
Duke of Lorraine in Nancy; the musicians and dancers who entertained

them in Nivelles and Louvain; the tennis court and jousting area in Nancy; the zoo in Parma. They averaged twenty five miles per day on horseback, a splendid average for men and women (the children were left in Flanders) in the inclement weather of February and March. On 14 April 1608 they reached Reggio from Piacenza in one day, a distance of over fifty miles. It was their 'longest day'.

The manoeuvering between Spain and the Papacy did not end with the arrival of the Earls in Rome. Henceforth the Spanish Ambassador in Rome is at the centre of the diplomacy, informing Philip III that the Pope is 'exceedingly parsimonious' and informing the Pope that 'in the present circumstances the King cannot openly send help to Ireland'. The ambassador quickly became an admirer of O Neill and pleaded with Philip III for an increased grant to the Earls, 'for the Pope has given them a house but not one stick of furniture and they have no money to buy such bare necessities as beds and chairs'. But as the years go by and O Neill's requests to Philip III are left unanswered or unheeded – for help for O Doherty's Rising in 1608, for help against the Ulster Plantation in 1609, for mediation in seeking reconciliation with King James I in 1608-10, for the restoration of his lands in 1612, for permission to move to Spain in 1612 and to Flanders in 1613 and 1614 – the plight of the exiled leader becomes pitiable in the extreme. His sons Hugh and Henry died in 1609 and 1610, Rory and Cathbharr O Donnell along with Maguire were already dead from 1608. His constant requests for military aid for Ireland were rejected by Spain. By 1614 Rome was being informed that King James I would moderate his harsh treatment of Irish Catholics if the Pope encouraged them to show loyalty to him. By that time, too, Archbishop Lombard was trying to work out a *modus vivendi* for the Catholic Church in Ireland with the new regime. O Neill had become a kind of 17th century Mindszenty. Ultimately he was told to remain quiet in Rome, otherwise his small monthly grant from Spain would be cut off.

Yet far from becoming the senile, blind, drunken, melancholic figure of some of his biographers, O Neill's mind remained alert and his hopes undimmed until the end. By 1614 he was planning his most determined effort to return to Ireland with Spanish aid. In March 1615 O Neill declared to the King of Spain that 'rather than live in Rome, he would prefer to go to his land with a hundred soldiers and die there in defence of the Catholic faith and of his fatherland'. His despatches to Spain became more militant in this year of the so-called 'Ulster Conspiracy', when several young Ulstermen, including O Neill's nephew, were executed on charges of plotting to release the Earl's youngest son, Conn, and other prisoners and seize several Ulster towns. As a precaution the boy was transferred from Charlemont to London and his father wrote defiantly to Velázquez of the Spanish Council of State in May 1615: 'A son of mine is even now being reared in heresy, but I trust in God that the blood he has in his veins will not permit such a deception, and that one day he will avenge for me this outrage'. Not the words of a broken man.

The last two letters of the collection are concerned with O Neill's death: approval from the Spanish Council of State for the Spanish

Ambassador's decision to pay his funeral expenses and for the transfer of
O Neill's monthly allowance to his wife. His tomb with its simple Latin
inscription in San Pietro in Montorio has been lost for nearly a century and
a half, a circumstance which does little credit to the Irish in Rome in the
middle of the last century who so passively accepted its disappearance. I
have recently sought permission to have some of the slabs in the flooring
removed in the hope that the inscription may be discovered. But even if his
monument is not traced, Micheline Kerney Walsh has raised a monument
as lasting as marble and more challenging than the bald statement on his
tomb. Simply by allowing the documents to speak for themselves she has
restored O Neill to his rightful place among the greatest of Irish leaders.

Tar éis dom an leabhar seo a léamh agus glór daingean Uí Néill a
chluinstin, deirim leis an bhanúdar mar a dúirt an file sa 17ú haois:

> Slán don mhnaoi bhí araoir ar uaigh Uí Néill,
> Le crá croí ag caoineadh uaisle Gael,
> Gí d'fhág sí mo chlí go suaite tréith,
> Mo ghrá í 's gach ní dá gcuala mé.

Ard Mhacha,
6 Bealtaine 1986.   + Tomás Ó Fiaich

Preface

This account of the exile of Hugh O Neill is the result of searches in Spanish archives over a period of many years. I first became interested in Hugh O Neill and his family some thirty years ago while working on the records of Spanish Military Orders in the Archivo Histórico Nacional at Madrid for the publication of *Spanish Knights of Irish Origin*. Among these records I came across much fascinating information on a son and a grandson of Hugh O Neill. His son, John, or Juan, was recognised in Spain as heir to his father's title of Earl of Tyrone, became colonel of an Irish regiment in Spanish service, was member of the Spanish Supreme Council of War and was killed at the siege of Barcelona in 1641.

Juan's son, Hugo Eugenio, was born in Madrid, out of wedlock, but was acknowledged by his father and was later legitimised by the Pope. The fate of the unfortunate mother is still a mystery. All that I could find out about her was that her name was Isabel O Donnell and that Juan O Neill 'could have married her because she was as noble as he, being a cousin of the Earl of Tyrconnell'. After the birth of her child she was placed in a convent, which she left shortly afterwards 'because the life did not suit her'.

Further searches, mainly in the archives at Simancas, gradually uncovered documents relating to Hugh O Neill himself and to his enforced exile in Rome, including his own letters to the King of Spain and his ministers. Most exciting of all, and last of the relevant documents which I came across, just as my funds for research were dwindling, was the very first letter sent by Hugh O Neill and his brother-in-law Ruairí O Donnell to the King of Spain after their perilous escape from Ireland. In this letter, written from Louvain in Spanish Flanders on 3 December 1607, they explain conditions in Ireland, the increasing difficulties of catholics under English rule and they appeal to King Philip for military aid with which they would return to Ireland to lead a planned rising, and they propose annexation to the Crown of Spain as a means of ending English domination in Ireland.

This work was first published by Cumann Seanchais Ard Mhacha, the Armagh Diocesan Historical Society, in 1986 under the title *Destruction by Peace, Hugh O Neill after Kinsale*. In the present edition I have made some slight changes in the text and, for greater ease of reading, most of the notes and the documents in the appendix of the first edition have been omitted.

I wish to express my gratitude to Dr. Eoin McKiernan of St. Paul, Minnesota, for his active encouragement in planning this publication.

Micheline Kerney Walsh

Introduction

Hugh O Neill, Earl of Tyrone and descendant of the ancient kings of Ireland, ranks among the great European figures of his day. At the height of his military successes his name was spoken in awe at the courts of Spain, the Low Countries, France, England, Scotland and the Vatican. With relatively small forces, he defeated the best generals that Queen Elizabeth of England was able to send against him, and for nine years he maintained a war which exhausted the resources of her treasury. King Henry IV of France, who took pride in his own military talent, called him 'the third soldier of his age', meaning that he himself was the first, and the Spanish general Count of Fuentes the second.

For an assessment of the role of this important figure in Irish history, because of the scarcity of our own native records we have had to rely mainly on English sources, which are naturally hostile to O Neill. This account of the last fourteen years of his life is based mainly on friendly continental sources, which go some way towards redressing the balance and provide us with much new information.

O Neill's rise to power was slow and deliberate. During the first half of his life he lived in the shadow of Queen Elizabeth's viceroys and ministers. It was not until the outbreak of the Nine Years' War in 1594 that he emerged openly as an enemy of the Crown.

The war of O Neill and his confederates, supported by intermittent help from Spain, against the forces of Queen Elizabeth of England ended with O Neill's submission in 1603. About this time, unknown to English authorities, O Neill sent messengers to Philip III of Spain, first to make known to him the reasons which had forced his submission and, later, to inform him of the increasingly difficult circumstances of Irish catholics and of his own worsening situation. Peace negotiations between Spain and England brought about a treaty, signed in London in August 1604, which put an end to Irish hopes of further open military support from Spain, but it seems that O Neill did not believe the peace would be of long duration. In December of that year his message to King Philip was that he and his confederates were prepared to wait up to two years, even in their difficult circumstances, to see what the King would 'wish to order for his service' in Ireland. Indeed, in those early years of uneasy peace it was the general opinion in diplomatic and government circles that hostilities would soon be renewed. Reports of the Spanish ambassador in London show that relations between the two countries came close to breaking point on several occasions and, in August 1606, the Earl of Nottingham, lord admiral of England and member of King James I's Privy Council, advised a merchant friend of his to withdraw his property from Spain, for it was his belief that the peace would not last three months. At the same time the French ambassador in London wrote to Paris:

> *It is my opinion that the English and the Spaniards are so dissimilar in all things, except in their excessive pride as regards which I know not who holds the advantage, that without any encouragement from us, it cannot be long before we see them come to grips again.*

In February of that same year of 1606, O Neill sent another message to King Philip stating that his position was becoming untenable. The English authorities, he claimed, had dispossessed him of a large part of his estates and had left on his lands many garrisons maintained at his expense. He no longer had even the means of maintaining his house or of 'bribing the heretics so as to gain them over' and his very life was threatened. His associate, Ruairí O Donnell, Earl of Tyrconnell, was in a similar position and, unless King Philip could send them financial aid by some secret means, they were resolved to escape with their lives and seek protection from the king, but they hoped this would not be necessary for if they were absent from Ireland when 'the opportunity arose, that country would be lost.' Presumably, the *opportunity* refers to a possible renewal of hostilities between England and Spain.

Clearly, O Neill had foreseen the possibility that circumstances might force him to seek refuge in Spain, but would have considered this only as a last resort. As is evident from his letters to King Philip, he calculated that a new rising against English domination, with some initial help from Spain, would have every chance of success because of the formation, in 1606, of a secret league between, on the one hand, O Neill and his confederates, and on the other, the catholics of the cities and of the Pale, who had previously sided with the forces of Queen Elizabeth and were now angered by the harsh measures taken against them by the ministers of King James. However, events took a different course and the timing of the departure of the Earls of Tyrone and Tyrconnell and their followers, now known as 'the Flight of the Earls', was determined by two factors; firstly, in the summer of 1607 O Neill had been summoned to London by King James and, secondly, while preparing to obey the summons, he received warning from certain friends of his on the English Privy Council that it was planned to have him arrested in London on a charge of high treason and executed. As O Neill explained to King Philip:

> *they warned us that, in order to save our lives, there was no other remedy but to take up arms, or to escape from the kingdom. We chose to escape rather than*

stir the whole kingdom to rebellion without first being assured of the help and assistance of Your Majesty.

Their departure was not merely an escape from arrest. O Neill planned to go to Spain and to make personal contact with King Philip whom he hoped to convince of the advantages, both religious and political, for Spain as well as for Ireland, of a military expedition designed to break English power in Ireland. Whether he would have succeeded, had he reached the King's presence, is impossible to tell, but it is certain that King James and his ministers were very fearful lest he would, and took extraordinary pains to prevent him from making personal contact with King Philip. As it happened, the Earls and their companions were forced by storms to land in France and, after much intriguing by English, Spanish and Papal diplomats and ministers, they eventually ended their journey in Rome, much against their wishes.

The plan of O Neill and of his supporters for the government of Ireland, had they succeeded in removing it from English control, is not clearly defined in any of their letters or memorials, but it is evident that they envisaged the annexation of Ireland to the Crown of Spain as the only means of retaining their lands and their religion against the power of England. Their attachment to their traditions and their way of life is expressed in a letter of O Neill and O Donnell to King Philip in December 1607, in which they describe Ireland as:

> *a kingdom consisting entirely of catholics . . . [who] have been on their domains from such ancient times that many of them, particularly ourselves, are lords of what we possessed up to the present, for the past two thousand years and more, and we have been so constant in the catholic faith that we have preserved it for the past thirteen hundred years despite the repeated attempts of the Danes and of the English to extinguish its flame.*

The idea of offering the crown of Ireland to Spain was not new; it had been proposed several times previously to Philip II and to his father, Charles V, and would have been acceptable to many of the Irish because of their belief in the Milesian tradition that the old Irish race was of Spanish origin. In the face of King James I of England's intolerance of the catholic religion, the idea became acceptable also to many of the old English catholics established in the cities and in the Pale; as early as June 1603 some of them had sent a representative to the King of Spain in the person of Guillermo Miagh, or William Meade, the Recorder of Cork. On the death of Queen Elizabeth in March of that year, Miagh had acted as leader of the citizens of Cork in attempting to obtain the free and public exercise of the catholic religion. After a term of imprisonment, he was forced into exile; later, in Spain, he played an important role as one of O Neill's representatives at the Spanish court. In the English State Papers relating to Ireland he is referred to as 'the reprobate Recorder of Cork'.

Undoubtedly, in the wake of a defeat of English forces in Ireland, the nomination of a Spanish prince as viceroy would have been expected; in May 1596 the northern chieftains had sent to King Philip the names of those who would be acceptable to them and the King's answer was that 'he had been very pleased with their suggestions but that it was early yet and the matter would be dealt with in good time.' After the 'Flight of the Earls', in one of the memorials in which O Neill put forward his plan for the reconquest of Ireland, he asked King Philip to appoint experienced and trustworthy Spaniards to accompany the expedition and to whom, O Neill writes: 'we should hand over, in the name of His Majesty, the castles and fortresses we capture'. That he did not aim to set himself up as king of Ireland, as is sometimes suggested, is evident from a letter of the Spanish Councillor Andrés Velázquez who had discussions with many of the Irish in Madrid, including O Neill's representatives, Archbishop Florence Conry and William Meade, and who wrote in 1615:

> *Although they have such great esteem for the Earl, they would not make him their king, for there are other catholics who only recognise him as their leader because of his personal talents and the fortunes of war and obey him willingly in wartime, but would not recognise him as their lord.*

Another interesting clue appears in the English State Papers. It is the report of a conversation held in January 1606 between an English captain, Sir Tobias Caulfield, and Bartholomew Owen, who was a close friend of O Neill's. Speaking of the Gunpowder Plot of November 1605 against King James, Caulfield suggested to Owen that, if it succeeded, O Neill would have sought to be king of Ireland:

> *No, said he* [Owen], *the Earl would have asked no more than his rightful inheritance which his ancestors enjoyed from the river Boyne* [recte: Bann] *to the Fynne at Lough Foyle with his Uriaghts* [i.e. subchiefs] *and that every other Lord should have governed his own country according to their ancient customs, that a Council of Estate should have been established of all the Earls and Lords of the countries and divers of the Barons of the Pale, and that they should have sovereign power, by a general consent to govern all, to hold correspondence with foreign princes, to decide all controversies and differences that might arise between the Lords of countries.*

With regard to O Neill's exile in Rome, until the discovery and publication of his correspondence with Spain it was generally assumed by modern historians and writers that he had accepted defeat and that, in despair, he had gone into voluntary exile. It was in his enemies' interest that such a view should be taken and that none in Ireland should entertain any hope of his return. Throughout the years of his exile, the English government and King James' ministers in Ireland were very fearful of the possibility of his return and of another uprising. Consequently they spread rumours designed to discourage his supporters in Ireland, as for instance the false rumour that O

Neill had become blind. Their propaganda was effective and was still felt in modern times when, until recently, virtually the only contemporary source material available for a study of that period was the English State Papers relating to Ireland. Based on these hostile sources, Sean O Faoláin in *The Great O Neill* has depicted a blind and despairing Hugh O Neill spending his last years in despondent and inactive defeatism and consoling himself with excessive drinking.

The picture which emerges from a study of Spanish sources is very different; it is that of a man of unbroken spirit, politically-minded, active and astute, with a clear grasp of contemporary international affairs. When it seemed politic to do so, O Neill suggested a reconciliation with King James and a peaceful restoration to his lands, but it is clear that his principal objective was always to return to Ireland at the head of an army, with the backing of Spain. The Spanish records tell in no uncertain way of the intrigues of King Philip, of his anxiety not to antagonise England by supporting too openly a man still regarded by the Spaniards as strong enough, even in defeat, to be one of England's most dangerous enemies. At the same time, King Philip and his advisers wished this recognised strength to be on their side should relations with England lead to open hostilities. Consequently, while O Neill's many requests to go to Spain to speak with the King were refused, he was kept in hope of Spanish aid when a favourable opportunity should arise.

Perhaps the most interesting sidelight on O Neill's qualities is the admiration of a man of the calibre of the Spanish ambassador, Francisco Ruiz de Castro, Conde de Castro and Duke of Taurisano, who knew O Neill more intimately than any other contemporary European. Castro was ambassador in Rome from 1609 to 1616, which was for most of O Neill's exile. On many occasions he risked the King's displeasure by pleading O Neill's cause against what he knew were the royal wishes. In 1610 he went so far as to refuse to convey to O Neill a reply from King Philip which the ambassador considered too curt; through the intermediary of the Secretary of State he succeeded in obtaining that the King reword his reply. Castro's esteem for O Neill is made clear in a letter of October 1612 in which he wrote to the King: 'The Earl is a great nobleman and Your Majesty owes much to his devotion and loyalty.'

A brief glance here at what is known of Hugh O Neill's early life may not be out of place. He was born in Dungannon in 1550; eight years earlier his grandfather, Conn O Neill, surnamed Bacach, or the lame one, chief of the O Neills of Tyrone, had considered it wise to come to an agreement with the King of England and had been created Earl of Tyrone by Henry VIII, with the title of Baron of Dungannon going to Conn's eldest son, Feardorcha, also referred to as Matthew, father of Hugh O Neill. There followed a family feud provoked by the contention of Conn's next son, Seán an Díomais, or Shane the Proud, that Feardorcha was illegitimate. In the course of this feud, in 1558, Feardorcha was killed, and Hugh O Neill's older brother, Brian, succeeded to the title of Baron of Dungannon. In 1559 Conn Bacach O Neill, Earl of Tyrone, died, bitterly regretting, it is said, his acceptance of an English title and cursing any of his descendants who would adopt English ways. The succession to his title was left undecided; by then Elizabeth I had come to the throne of England and English policy in Ireland was, as the historian O Sullivan Beare puts it, to 'fan dissensions among Irish chiefs' and to support the weaker party against the stronger, thus ensuring that none should become too powerful an opponent to the Queen's government in Dublin which was gradually extending its area of control. Also in 1559, Shane the Proud had been inaugurated by his people chief of the O Neills of Tyrone in succession to his father. The new English viceroy, the Earl of Sussex, supported the young Baron of Dungannon, Brian O Neill, against his uncle, but Brian was killed in 1561, a victim of the continuing feud, and his title devolved upon his younger brother, Hugh O Neill.

After the death of his father, Hugh was made a ward of the Crown and was brought up in the Pale under the guardianship of Giles Hovendon. In a later reference to this period of his life, O Neill mentions his 'education amongst the English'. The mistaken assumption that he received his education in England was corrected by Hiram Morgan in his recent work entitled *Tyrone's Rebellion*.

In 1567 O Neill paid what appears to have been his first visit to the English court, returning in 1568 to his barony and to his grandfather's castle of Dungannon. To all appearances the process of anglicisation was complete and Hugh O Neill was given the command of a troop of cavalry: he attended parliament in Dublin, fought for the Earl of Essex and served under the Queen's banner during the Desmond rebellion. In 1585 he received the title of Earl of Tyrone and shortly afterwards was put in possession of most of the territory of Tyrone, which was of far greater extent than the modern county of that name. However, by 1588, Queen Elizabeth's ministers in Dublin were beginning to doubt the loyalty of the new Earl of Tyrone because he had helped Spanish survivors of the Armada.

The following year he was accused by Aodh Geimhleach O Neill, a son of Shane the Proud, of having correspondence with the King of Spain and with the Scots who were at war with England. When it became known that the Earl was responsible for the death of Aodh Geimhleach, he was summoned to Dublin where he denied having correspondence with enemies of the Crown and insisted on going to London to justify the killing of Aodh Geimhleach. To the lords of the Privy Council in London he admitted that he had not acted in accordance with English law, but he declared that Aodh Geimhleach had been guilty of several crimes and that, according to the ancient form of government in Ulster, he was entitled to order the execution of evil-doers. Having promised for the future to observe English law and customs, the Earl returned to Ireland in August 1590, but not before he had obtained permission to import lead for the restoration of the roof of his castle; however, the lead was to serve a different purpose, for it was used eventually as ammunition during the war against Queen Elizabeth.

In the winter of 1591 the Earl of Tyrone's young brother-in-law, Red Hugh O Donnell, escaped from Dublin Castle where he had been imprisoned and held hostage for four years by the English viceroy. On his return to Ulster after his dramatic escape, he visited O Neill, at the latter's request, and spent several days with him. Shortly afterwards Edmund MacGauran, Archbishop of Armagh, returned from Spain with assurances that King Philip would be willing to assist an Irish rebellion. From then on, events moved gradually towards open war, though it was not until 1595 that the Earl of Tyrone took the field and gained his first victory over Queen Elizabeth's forces at Clontibret in May of that year. In June he was proclaimed a traitor by order of the Queen and, three months later, following the death of the old chieftain, Turlough Luineach, the Earl was inaugurated chief of the O Neills of Tyrone.

O Neill and O Donnell appealed to Spain for aid of troops, arms and munitions; some early messages to and from Spain were intercepted or, because of shipwreck, failed to reach their destination, but eventually contact was established and messengers from Spain brought arms, money and promises of more substantial help. Early in 1596 King Philip, anxious that the Irish should not make peace with England, wrote to O Neill and his confederates exhorting them to continue the war. So anxious, indeed, was the King that his message should reach its destination that he had triplicate copies of his letters sent to Ireland by three ships, each of which sailed from a different port: Lisbon, La Coruña and Santander. The captains of the ships were given instructions regarding what they were to say to the Irish chiefs on behalf of the King and, though they were to encourage them and give them good hope of assistance:

> *so that they should not come to terms with the enemy who, they say, is making them great offers to that end; neither should they act hastily and attack the enemy before the time, thereby causing their destruction and denying us the opportunity of helping them.*

The three ships arrived safely and O Neill sent back assurances that, despite the truce which had been declared and was still in being, he would not conclude peace with England. One of these messengers from Spain, Captain Alonso de Cobos, returned again to Ireland in September 1596 bringing letters from King Philip for the northern chieftains and announcing the arrival of a Spanish fleet before the winter. His account of the journey and of his meeting with the Irish is translated in the *Calendar of State Papers, Spain,* edited by the English historian Martin Hume; however, there are several inaccuracies in the translation and one grave error should be pointed out, for it contradicts the meaning of the original and does an injustice to O Neill and to Captain Cobos. The Captain reports that, having heard that the Earl of Tyrone had sent to the English General Norris a letter from King Philip to the Earl, which the Captain had brought on his previous journey, he asked O Neill and O Donnell why this had been done. The Earl explained that the English authorities had known of the arrival of the Spanish ships at the coast of Donegal and had accused him of double dealing, for the truce was still in being and, in order to convince them and so as not to risk renewing the war before the time, he had sent the letter, having received a promise that it would be returned. Despite his promise, the General did not return the letter and eventually it was sent to London. In view of this, Cobos continues:

> *I told them to consider how he [the English general] would keep his word in other circumstances when it might be of importance to the Queen that it be broken, since he acted in this manner with regard to returning a letter after reading it.*

In other words, Cobos advised O Neill and O Donnell not to trust the promises of the English general for the future.

In the Calendar the incorrect version of this passage is: *I warned them [O Neill and O Donnell] to keep their promises better for the future.* This implied mistrust of O Neill and O Donnell, wrongly attributed to the Spaniard, is emphasized by a repetition of the sentence in the Introduction to the Calendar, p. lxi. More recently, Hume's inaccurate translation has been copied and embellished by Cyril Falls in his book entitled *Elizabeth's Irish Wars,* pp. 197 and 198, in which he has Cobos *reproving* O Neill and *firmly* warning him to keep his promises better for the future. The contents of the King's letter were of no great significance for it was written in general terms, messages of importance being usually transmitted by word of mouth and, apparently, it had the desired effect in Dublin.

The instructions which Philip II gave to Captain Cobos with regard to his dealings with the Irish leaders contain an interesting reference to the sack of Cádiz by an English fleet, which had taken place in June of that year. The King had rightly assumed that Queen Elizabeth's ministers in Ireland would make much of their success at Cádiz so as to discourage the Irish leaders and reduce them to obedience; indeed, the Captain's report of his meeting with the northern chiefs contains the following account:

> *Those gentlemen asked me what the English fleet had done in Spain because the enemy had told them they had sacked Cádiz and many other places, taken many galleons, burned a fleet, carried away much plunder and many prisoners, burned down many places and had done much else of note without hindrance from anyone in Spain.*

Captain Cobos reassured them and told them, as he had been instructed to do, that the English had indeed raided Cádiz but that their account of this was much exaggerated. He gave them the Spanish view of the event and assured them, on the King's behalf, that it would make no difference to the expedition which he had planned to send to Ireland. The promised expedition, composed of 100 ships, sailed from Lisbon in October 1596, but a storm off the coast of Spain caused such loss and damage that the survivors were forced to return to port. Another attempt was made the following year when a fleet of 160 ships left the port of Ferrol on 19 October 1597. Once again the fleet was scattered by a storm and suffered heavy losses.

In Ireland, the early successes of O Neill and his associates at Clontibret, Monaghan and elsewhere, during the campaign of 1595, had the effect not only of increasing the ranks of their supporters, but also of frightening the Dublin government of Queen Elizabeth into proposing peace negotiations. The truce which was made in October of that year was prolonged throughout 1596.

The arrival of a new Viceroy, Lord Burgh, in May 1597, marked the renewal of hostilities, but the armies with which he attempted to invade Ulster were roundly defeated on the Blackwater, at Tyrrellspass and on the Erne. O Neill's military tactics and his control and distribution of the forces at his disposal had been completely successful. Burgh survived the campaign but died of illness before the year was out, and the same fate befell the English General Norris.

The following year saw O Neill's greatest victory of the war. An English garrison at Portmore, the Blackwater fort in O Neill's territory, was besieged from early summer and was still holding out at the end of July. Sir Henry Bagenal, brother-in-law and sworn enemy of O Neill, set out from Newry at the head of over 4,000 men to relieve the fort and bring supplies to the starving garrison. On 14 August 1598, O Neill, assisted by O Donnell and Maguire, led an attack on Bagenal at the Yellow Ford, between Armagh and Portmore, and defeated him, with a loss of nearly half his force. Bagenal himself was killed and the broken remains of his army returned to Armagh, having lost the greater part of its guns and equipment.

O Neill's prestige soared and the panic-stricken government in Dublin found itself unable to suppress the movement of support for him which spread throughout the country. Such evident success should have encouraged immediate supportive action from King Philip against Queen Elizabeth, Spain's most dangerous enemy, but, while these events were taking place, Philip II lay in his palace of the Escorial, afflicted with a miserably long and painful illness, of which he died on September 13th 1598.

The new king, Philip III, sent promises of help to Ireland, but other matters took precedence with him. Eventually an expedition was prepared under the command of Don Juan del Aguila, consisting of a force of 4,500 men and 33 ships, which sailed from Lisbon in September 1601, most of which landed at Kinsale. While awaiting the arrival of Spanish aid, O Neill had gained time by alternating military successes with parleys and truces; in this manner he succeeded in conserving his strength for a considerable time, but the momentum had been lost. By 1601, he was no longer in the strong position he had reached after his resounding victory at the battle of the Yellow Ford in August 1598 and, as he pointed out to King Philip:

> *The help which Your Majesty sent us and for which we had waited so many years, came to land in the province of Munster, so far from our own lands that we had to march one hundred leagues in the depth of winter, through enemy country, crossing many rivers and forced to make many bridges, in order to go to the aid of those whom Your Majesty had sent to help us. There [at Kinsale], God permitting, we suffered a misfortune which obliged us to return again to our lands and to send our brother, the Earl O Donel, who is in glory, to beg Your Catholic Majesty to send us further help.*

According to the contemporary Irish historian, Philip O Sullivan Beare:

> *O Neill, who, after the loss he had sustained, was no weaker, wished to continue the war against the enemy in the old way, but he was wholly unable to get his followers to agree to this. For O Rorke returned to defend his country against his brother . . . Ranald [MacDonnell] followed suit, and others were influenced by their example, and forced O Neill also to retire, much against his will.*

The ease with which O Neill and his troops returned north after their defeat at Kinsale is the subject of interesting comments in the State Papers of England and of Spain. From Dublin, on 12 January 1602, the lord Chancellor and Privy Councillors wrote to the lords of the Privy Council of England:

> *We greatly grieve that such an archtraitor should have been able to go . . . back again to the north without any stop or hindrance.*

A possible explanation is supplied in the report of the Spanish Captain Diego de Cuenca who returned from Ireland in June 1602:

> *When the Earl Onel retreated, the enemy followed him with some troops, but he had an easy passage because he spread the word that he had beaten the enemy and that Don Juan del Aguila and the Earl Odonel were on their way to besiege Cork, and so he passed freely until he reached his lands.*

CHAPTER ONE

After Kinsale

On the evening of the Sunday following the battle of Kinsale, while O
Neill and his troops were retreating to the north, Red Hugh O Donnell set
out for Spain to seek further help. The revised calendar of Pope Gregory
XIII which was followed by Spain and by the Irish catholics was not
adopted by England until many years later, consequently the battle of
Kinsale is recorded in the English State Papers as having occurred during
the night of 24 - 25 December 1601, whereas, according to Spanish and
Irish reckoning it took place during the night of 3 - 4 January 1602, a
discrepancy of ten days. Unless otherwise stated, the dates mentioned in
this study are those which accord with the Gregorian calendar.

On 6 January 1602, Red Hugh O Donnell sailed from Castlehaven
in the ship of the Spanish general, Don Pedro de Zubiaur, who was
returning to Spain with letters for King Philip from Don Juan del Aguila
and others. Among those who accompanied O Donnell were the Franciscan, Father Florence Conry, afterwards Archbishop of Tuam, Father
Maurice Dunleavy of the same order, from the monastery of Donegal, the
Baron of Leitrim, Raymond Burke, who figured prominently in the war
and who later applied to join the Dominicans at Lisbon, and Captain
Hugh Mostian who, as we are informed by the historian O Sullivan Beare,
was the son of an English father and of an Irish mother. Mostian had been
the Queen's governor of Athenry and had served with the English forces
until 1597 when, as he declared to Philip III some years later:

> *Considering that the war in Ireland was justified, that it was approved by
> His Holiness and encouraged by Your Majesty, he left his governorship and the
> salary which he received from the Queen, and also his lands and possessions, in
> order to defend the holy catholic faith and to serve Your Majesty. Then, the
> Archbishop of Dublin, Don Mateo de Oviedo, and Don Martin de la Cerda
> received his oath that he would serve Your Majesty all his life.*

On 13 January, O Donnell and his companions landed at Luarca on
the coast of Asturias after so stormy a passage that Zubiaur declared it was
as much as they could do to save their lives. O Donnell, anxious to lose no
time, wanted to set out immediately for the court at Valladolid; but at that

time the King and his court were on a tour of the province of León, and so
O Donnell and his party accompanied Zubiaur on the journey overland to
La Coruña, there to await the King's summons. Philip III was then a
young man of twenty-three years of age and, by all accounts, he was a
good and virtuous man; he was very pious, had profound reverence for all
things religious and never drank wine. According to the famous contemporary author, Quevedo, 'he lived for others and died for God'. But he
was weak and ineffectual; his lack of understanding of, and his lack of
interest in the affairs of the world and of his country caused him to
delegate his power and authority to the flamboyant, ambitious and
unscrupulous Duke of Lerma who, during his twenty years of favour
with the King, enriched his family at the expense of the state and amassed
a personal fortune of over forty million ducats.

At La Coruña, O Donnell and his companions were welcomed by
that great friend of the Irish, the Conde de Caracena, governor of Galicia,
who offered them the hospitality of his own house. We are told by an
Englishman who visited La Coruña three years later that the governor's
house was: 'the whole pleasure of the town, for that it overlooketh the
whole harbour and is seated in the heart of the town.'

In the meantime, Zubiaur's dispatches from Luarca had reached the
King and on 29 January, at Valdavido in the province of León, a Junta
composed of the Duke of Lerma, the Marqués de Velada, the Secretary
Don Juan de Idiaquez, and the King's confessor, Fray Gaspar de Córdoba,
considered the letters and reports from Ireland which brought the news of
the defeat at Kinsale and of the difficult situation of the Spaniards besieged
in the town. Having discussed the means of sending promptly the help
required by Don Juan del Aguila, they submitted their recommendations
to the King and added:

> *Since the Earl Odonel is already here, it would be convenient that Your*
> *Majesty should hear him before returning to Valladolid, and that he should be*
> *ordered to come to one of the places on the way. When Your Majesty has heard*
> *him, consoled him and shown him favour, he should return to La Coruña to be*
> *ready to sail with the help which will leave from that port.*

Word was sent to O Donnell to join the court at Zamora, some four
hundred kilometres south-east of La Coruña, and he set out on his journey
accompanied by Father Florence Conry, the Baron of Leitrim, Captain
Mostian and nine other Irish gentlemen, with an escort provided by the
Conde de Caracena. He was received by King Philip and the councillors,
to whom he explained the purpose of his mission and put forward his
request for aid to Ireland. On 13 February, the Council of State held a
meeting as a result of which, that same evening, the Secretary Don Pedro
Franqueza sent the following report to the Duke of Lerma:

> *The Council is of the opinion that grateful acknowledgement be offered to*

the Earl Odonel for the zeal and good will he shows for the service of His Majesty and he should be given assurances that His Majesty will act towards him and Onel and the catholics of Ireland in the same manner as if they were his vassals and that, without delay, he will order the assembly of the troops which will be needed to assist Don Juan [del Aguila], should he still be holding out, in which case they will disembark in the place which he advises. Should the greater number of troops, which he mentions, be sent, they also will disembark where he advises. This army of support will be assembled at Lisbon and at La Coruña and, so that he may see what is being done and that he may keep Onel informed, His Majesty has resolved that he should go to Lisbon or to La Coruña, leaving the choice to him, and, wherever he may choose to go, His Majesty will take due care of him and will provide him and his people with all things necessary and, from the place to which he will choose to go, he will be in a position to send his views according as they occur to him. For the journey he should be given one thousand ducats.

The Council also decided upon the most effective means of assembling a force of six thousand men in the ports of Lisbon and La Coruña and advised that 20 March should be fixed as the date by which all should be ready. On 23 February, Lerma replied that the King had seen Franqueza's report and that he agreed with all the recommendations of the Council.

Apart from his official mission, O Donnell had another more personal favour to ask of the King. He wanted to see his young nephew, the fifteen-year-old Henry O Neill who was then a student at the University of Salamanca. Henry was the second son of Hugh O Neill, Earl of Tyrone, by his second wife, Siobhán O Donnell, sister of Red Hugh. He had left Ireland at the end of April 1600, sent by his father, with the approval of King Philip, to be educated in Spain. The following year he had caused quite a stir in Spanish diplomatic circles by taking the Franciscan habit. Being a son of Spain's strongest ally in Ireland and a minor, whose education and welfare had been guaranteed in Spain by both King and Council, this move, without his father's expressed approval or knowledge, was discussion matter for several meetings of the Council of State, and it was not long before Henry was persuaded to give up the Franciscan habit. When he was summoned to meet his uncle at Zamora, he was nearing the end of his studies at Salamanca and he obtained his degree in Arts the following July.

Having spent less than a week at Zamora, O Donnell returned to La Coruña where he arrived on 26 February. It is probable that, on the way, he passed the messenger carrying to the court the news of Don Juan del Aguila's surrender at Kinsale, for the news had reached La Coruña on the previous day. At any rate, on his arrival, O Donnell would have heard the news from Caracena, which, judging from the Council's report of 13 February quoted above, cannot have been unexpected. On 22 January, del Aguila had signed articles of capitulation by which he surrendered to the

English not only Kinsale but also the O Sullivan castle of Dunboy and the
O Driscoll castles at Baltimore and Castlehaven. In a letter which O
Donnell addressed to King Philip two days after his return to La Coruña he
makes no mention of these events at Kinsale, but it is of particular interest
to note his tone of direct and personal approach to the King, bearing in
mind that he had just had contact with Philip and with Lerma, whose
influence over the King was so well known and of whom the Papal Nuncio
wrote to Cardinal Aldobrandini: 'He is the only one by whom His Majesty
is led and, whoever does not approach, the King through him, does
business badly or late – *negocia mal o tarde.*   But perhaps O Donnell felt
that, at Zamora, he had succeeded in engaging the King's attention and so,
on 28 February, he wrote to Philip:

> *Señor, all that we know concerning Ireland we wrote down for the
> Council. In this letter we merely beg Your Majesty with all humility to be
> pleased to give attention to this matter, for, since I have seen the royal presence of
> Your Majesty, we have more confidence in you for the benefit and advancement
> of our poor country, than in the whole world; and, provided the matter is
> attended to with the required haste, I pledge my word to Your Royal Majesty
> that, once landed there, we shall make the whole country subject to Your
> Majesty in a very short time. This I promise, knowing the state of the country at
> present. May God keep Your Majesty for many long years. From La Coruña
> on the last day of February 1602.*
>
> *Aodh O Domhnaill.*

It has been generally accepted by modern historians that, after del
Aguila's surrender at Kinsale, a fresh Spanish expedition was never seriously contemplated; however, there is much evidence to the contrary in
Spanish contemporary records and it is clear that King Philip decided upon
a second expedition to Ireland with a much larger force than that which
had landed at Kinsale in September 1601. Perhaps the young chieftain of
Donegal had imparted some of his energy to the usually apathetic Philip; at
any rate it was decided, when the situation was re-assessed after the
surrender at Kinsale, that a force of fourteen thousand men, more than
three times the strength of the Kinsale expedition, was to be collected at
Lisbon where a fleet of sixty-seven ships would also assemble and, when
the time came, Philip himself would go to Lisbon to give encouragement
to his army and to witness the departure of his fleet. Even details of the
royal progress from Valladolid to Lisbon were discussed.   Meanwhile,
munitions, arms and money were to be sent to Ireland and, on 16 March
1602, the King had written to his ambassador in Flanders instructing him
to inform the Archduke Albert, governor of Spanish Flanders, of plans for
the Irish expedition and to ask him to send to Spain certain Irish officers of
experience from the army of Flanders who were to join O Neill in
Ireland.   The commander appointed for the proposed expedition was

Don Martín de Padilla, Adelantado de Castilla. When he died suddenly in May, King Philip immediately appointed a replacement in the person of Don Juan de Cardona to whom he wrote on 27 May:

> *For the service of God, for the cause of religion and for the sake of my reputation which is at stake in this expedition, I desire in the extreme that you should overcome all difficulties which might prevent its success.*

On 5 June, lengthy instructions were forwarded to Cardona, signed by the Secretary Don Pedro de Franqueza who explained that the King was resolved to send to Ireland:

> *an army of such strength that, if the friendly* [Irish] *forces were not able to join it, it would be sufficient not only to restore the Earls* [O Neill and O Donnell] *and the Lords of the said castles* [O Sullivan and the O Driscolls] *to the state in which they were before the expedition of Don Juan* [del Aguila] *but also to render them more powerful so that, without other aid, they may reduce that kingdom to our holy faith and religion, which is the principal aim of His Majesty in this enterprise.*

The King and his Council considered that such a large expeditionary force would ensure success and they decided against sending a smaller force in the meantime in order to avoid a recurrence of the Kinsale disaster. In coming to these decisions, they had overlooked the urgency of the situation in Ireland and the length of time it would take to assemble a force of the size envisaged. In April, O Donnell had written pressingly to the King asking for a force of two thousand men, or even one thousand, with which he would return to Ireland and keep the war alive until the arrival of the main fleet. His plan, forwarded in writing with his letter, was to land on the coast of Donegal, fortify Killybegs, Donegal and a post on Lough Foyle, then lay siege to Galway; he argued that:

> *even if the Queen had 16,000 troops, the passes through which they would be forced to come to the relief of the city are so bad and narrow that they can be defended by 3,000 Irishmen; nor can the city be relieved by sea, because large ships do not reach within cannon shot of the city. Their cargo is brought in by boats which go along a river running from the city to the sea.*

In June O Donnell repeated his request and he and Father Conry, supported by Caracena, wrote not only now to King Philip, but also to the Duke of Lerma, representing the necessity of immediate help to the Irish who were still in arms. But the King, fearful of further possible loss of prestige, was now thinking in terms of a great army. From his ministers he had received the following recommendation:

> *The Council has already represented to Your Majesty that it is not advisable to send a small army to the catholics of Ireland because of the manifest danger of defeat, as experience has shown, and the consequent grave damage to*

the reputation of Your Majesty.

From the Escorial, on 20 June, King Philip sent to the Conde de Caracena a long letter of instructions regarding preparations and supplies for the large fleet which was being assembled and asked to be informed of any news coming from Ireland. In conclusion, he wrote:

> *You will tell the Earl Odonel that very soon he will understand how attentive I am with regard to his consolation and help and to that of the Earl Onel and the Irish catholics.*

While these preparations were going ahead, O Neill had retreated to his northern territories with depleted forces and continued to hold out while awaiting news from Spain, and Mountjoy, Queen Elizabeth's Lord Deputy in Ireland, was reassembling his own weakened resources in readiness for a campaign against O Neill. Charles Blount, Lord Mountjoy, had been appointed Deputy, or Viceroy, early in 1600; he arrived in Dublin late in February of that year, determined to succeed where his predecessor, Essex, had failed and had fallen into disgrace. According to Mountjoy's secretary, Fynes Moryson, 'Hee much affected glory and honour, and had a great desire to raise his house... His desire of honour and hope of reward and advancement by the warres, yea of returning to retiredness after the warres ended, made him hotly imbrace the forced course of the warre . . .' He was to succeed in his purpose and, when he returned to London in 1603 after the end of the war and the death of Queen Elizabeth, he was appointed to King James' Privy Council and was created Earl of Devonshire. Fynes Moryson tells us that Mountjoy had been 'in his youth addicted to Popery' and it is interesting to find that, among those of his relatives whom the Deputy brought with him to Ireland, was one Captain James Blount, a catholic who, later in Spain, declared that he took advantage of his position 'by constantly giving information to the catholic Earls O Neill and O Donnell regarding all the enemy plans and movements'. During the last few months of 1602, Captain Blount, with his company, was based at Mountjoy Fort on the south-western shore of Lough Neagh.

In Spain, in February 1602, King Philip received information that Mountjoy had issued a proclamation offering a reward of two thousand marks for O Neill's head and two thousand pounds to any who would capture him alive. At the same time Mountjoy wrote to the lords of the Privy Council in London:

> *It is most sure that never Traitor knew better how to keepe his owne head, then this, nor any Subjects have a more dreadfull awe to lay violent hands on their sacred Prince, then these people have to touch the person of their O Neales.*

The proclamation had no effect and, four months later, King Philip was informed that it had been renewed and the amount offered increased to the sum of two thousand pounds for O Neill's head and three thousand pounds alive. On 17 June 1602, the lords of the Council at Dublin wrote to Sir George Carew, President of Munster:

> *Before the Lord Deputy's departure hence, it was agreed upon by his Lordship and Council that proclamation should be made denouncing head money for the arch-traitor Tyrone; which being put in print we have of them sent your Lordship herewith ten, praying your Lordship to see them forthwith published in the cities, market towns and other public places of that province."*

No copy of the printed proclamation appears to have survived. In England, Queen Elizabeth and her ministers, their confidence restored by the recent defeat of the Spaniards, appeared to attach little importance to the reports of English spies who sent repeated warnings of Spanish preparations for an expedition to Ireland. Nevertheless, an English fleet was dispatched to keep watch on the coast of Spain. In Ireland, the President of Munster, Sir George Carew, was not satisfied with the reassurance sent to him from London and viewed with dismay the weakness of his garrisons and of his defences. From Shandon, on 11 August 1602, he wrote to the Earl of Thomond, Donogh O Brien, who was then in England; O Brien had been reared at the court of Queen Elizabeth and had fought consistently on the English side throughout the war:

> *The bearer, Sir Anthony Cooke, will tell you of all things here, and of our expectation of the Spaniards. To be short, for God's sake come away for I am of opinion, make all the haste you may, the Don Diegoes with their great breeches will be here before you. Every day brings me news from one port or another that they are coming for Ireland, and most of them for Munster and some precisely for Cork. I have sent all this news to Court and to the Lord Deputy; and if they think the reports are true I am sure they will not leave me unsupplied; but urge the sending of supplies I dare not, lest, if the Spaniards do not come, I shall be charged with drawing the Queen to needless expense, and hindering the Northern prosecution which, by reports, seems to be brought to an end. Modestly, however, I entreat you to bring aids. The Lord Deputy is so far off and his army so scattered, that he cannot reassemble and come to me in a month after the enemy is landed. I must hold Cork, Kinsale and Haleboline. The two forts are not made, nor will be tenable in a long time. I am nominally 2,400 foot, but, sick etc. deducted, have not above 2,000 men. How I can defend many places with such a force against a powerful enemy you know, and, as you will be listened to there, please let your opinion on the matter be known.*

At this time, the Lord Deputy Mountjoy was in Newry, on his way, as he wrote from that town on 12 August, to take the field against O Neill and, he added, 'we are very glad that the Queen will send us 2,000 foot, for we need that number at least to fill up our weak companies.'

If, even then, a Spanish army of only two thousand men had landed in Ireland, as O Donnell had asked, events might have taken a different course; but it was not to be expected that the large force which the King envisaged could be assembled in a short time. At the end of July 1602 it became clear that the fleet would not be ready to sail before the stormy weather of autumn, and the King wrote to Caracena that the large amount of supplies which he had ordered would not now be necessary because 'the galleys and the infantry which were expected from Italy have been delayed so much that it will not be possible this year to achieve the purpose which was intended.' The ships which had been made ready at La Coruña were now ordered to set out to meet and escort the treasure fleet coming from New Spain, the West Indies and Brazil.

O Donnell had been asking insistently to be allowed to return to the court so as to discuss the situation with the King and his council: finally, permission was granted and, on 2 August, Caracena wrote to King Philip that O Donnell would leave La Coruña on the following Monday, August 5th, and would go to Simancas as the King had ordered. The distance between La Coruña and Valladolid, about 450 kilometres, was covered regularly in five days by the post, and the royal castle of Simancas is just eleven kilometres west of Valladolid. It is probable that O Donnell arrived at Simancas on 10 August; he died there on 10 September after an illness which lasted seventeen days. He may have been poisoned by the now notorious James Blake, or Blacadell, of Galway, but, if so, the fact was unsuspected by O Donnell's closest contemporaries. Father Florence Conry who was with him during his illness and at his death makes no mention of that possibility in his letters and memorials; neither does Hugh O Neill, who states, however, that between 1604 and 1607 several attempts were made to kill himself and some of his associates by poison. The case against Blake rests upon a letter of the English President of Munster, Sir George Carew, who, writing from Cork on 28 May 1602 (old style), reports a conversation with Blake as follows:

> *After much speech, protesting innocency and integrity, to clear himself of all suspicion, he took a solemn oath to do service that should merit good opinion and reward . . . I applauded his enterprise, whereupon he departed from me, and is gone into Spayne with a determination (bound with many oaths) to kyll O Donnell. That he is gone I am sure by those that were ymbarked with 'him. God give him strength and perseverance .*

Blake was probably a double agent and his 'career of adventure, double-dealing and treachery' is well described by Frederick M. Jones in an article based on material in the Vatican Archives and in the English State Papers. Spanish records offer us yet more information concerning him. In 1588 he had helped survivors of the Spanish Armada, for which he was imprisoned by the English authorities in Ireland. Later, in Spain, in recognition of his services he was given a pension of 40 crowns a month. In 1593 he was serving with the Spanish army in Brittany. In 1595 he was sending information to Queen Elizabeth's Secretary of State, Lord Burghley, but was reported to be dissatisfied with the payment. In 1597 a Limerick merchant arrived in Spain with a message to King Philip from Blake who offered to give help, should the Spanish fleet which was being prepared land in Ireland. At the same time, it was reported he was still in correspondence with Burghley; nevertheless he was still suspect to Queen Elizabeth's ministers and was imprisoned in Dublin Castle where he spent three years. He was released, as he claimed, through the influence of Sir Christopher Blount who was marshal of the English army in Ireland during the Earl of Essex's term of office as Viceroy. He was imprisoned again in Galway in 1601 but managed to escape shortly after the defeat of Kinsale. He then made his way to Cork where he had the interview with George Carew, whose report has branded him as the poisoner of Red Hugh O Donnell.

It is difficult to reconcile the varied and contradictory accounts of Blake, but it is certain that he was suspected of spying by the Spanish, by the English and by the Irish, and that he was imprisoned in Spain as well as in Ireland. One could almost have sympathy for him when he wrote from a Spanish prison:

> *For my sins, I am punished in Ireland because of the Spaniards, and in Spain I am suspected of being English. It is a most pitiful and painful condition and it would seem that my whole life has been very badly employed .*

Blake would appear to have been extremely plausible, talented and quick-witted, though somewhat unbalanced; however, on the evidence available up to the present, it is not certain that he was responsible for the death of O Donnell. He arrived in Lisbon in May 1602 and, when his presence there became known, several of the Irish exiles, including the Bishop of Killaloe, Cornelius O Mulrian, and Red Hugh O Donnell himself, warned the King's ministers of their suspicion that James Blake who, when in Spain, signed Diego Blacadell, was a spy. The following note is headed: 'From the Earl O Donnell'. It is undated and unsigned, and was probably forwarded by Caracena to a member of the Council of State around June 1602:

> *The Señor O Donell has heard that an Irish gentleman called Diego Blaccadel has landed at Lisbon with some messages from the Irish chiefs for His Majesty and for himself. Considering that this gentleman has been a prisoner of the English for some time and that he sailed from Cork, which is the worst place of the kingdom, ruled by the most perverse governor of any, he wishes that your lordship would write to the Court warning them not to trust this person with any secret information regarding the fleet and the army for Ireland, until the arrival*

of the Señor O Donell himself or of Fray Florencio, his confessor. He believes this will be of benefit to the service of His Majesty.

Despite the fact that Blake had no written messages or recommendations from the Irish chiefs, the Spanish governor at Lisbon sanctioned his journey to the court at Valladolid. There, on 29 August, while a few miles away Red Hugh O Donnell had already been stricken with his final illness, Blake presented to the Duke of Lerma a plan for the capture of Galway by a Spanish expeditionary force of 2,000 men who, he specified, 'should be subject to my guidance during the undertaking'. It is curious, to say the least, that in this document he makes no reference whatsoever to the presence in Spain of Red Hugh O Donnell who had travelled to the court on a similar mission and was then lying ill at Simancas; there is only one vague mention of the Donegal chieftain when Blake describes the situation of Galway: 'not far distant are O Neill and O Donnell and all their allied chieftains and knights. One wonders if, a fortnight later, he joined O Donnell's funeral cortège on its way to Valladolid for burial in the Franciscan church of that city. According to Lughaidh O Clery the body of the Donegal chieftain was taken from Simancas 'in a four-wheeled hearse with great numbers of State officers, of the Council and of the royal guard all round it, with blazing torches and bright flambeaux of beautiful waxlights blazing all round on each side of it.'

Blake and his servant, Robert Kirwan, were arrested shortly afterwards and were questioned extensively in the prison of Valladolid in November 1602 and again in December of that year; they were then aged forty and twenty-three respectively. It is clear from the questions put to them that Blake was not suspected of having anything to do with O Donnell's death. In answer to one of the questions, he admitted having spoken to the President of Munster before leaving Ireland but, when asked the purpose of his visit to the President, he replied that MacWilliam Burke had sent him to negotiate a truce of one or two months, which he had not been able to obtain and that, in Cork, he took ship secretly for Spain. In one of his more interesting statements, this extraordinary man declares that he acted as intermediary between O Neill and the Earl of Essex when, as he claims, they were planning a rising against the Queen of England:

Asked if he [Blake] *returned to England, and for what reason . . . he answered that it is true he went to England about one or two years ago, and the reason was that the Earl of Essex, the same who raided Cadiz, had dealings with the Prince Onel of Ireland about causing a rising against the Queen of England, for which reason he was beheaded in England, and the said Earl employed the deponent* [i.e. Blake] *as intermediary between himself and the said Prince .*

In fact, in September 1599, Essex, then Viceroy in Ireland, had agreed to a parley with O Neill, following which a truce was declared. Essex returned to England, was censured for his mismanagement of the campaign in Ireland, accused of plotting treason with O Neill, and was executed in February 1601.

Without supporting evidence, one would hesitate to accept Blake's statement, yet it does not contradict what little is known of the possibility of a plot between O Neill and Essex. A letter written to Philip III by the Spanish Archbishop of Dublin, Mateo de Oviedo, relates what O Neill had told him concerning the matter. Mateo made several journeys to Ireland as Philip's envoy to the northern chiefs before joining the Kinsale expedition. His letter, written from the Franciscan monastery of Donegal on 24 April 1600, relates that O Neill had almost persuaded Essex to leave the service of Queen Elizabeth and to join that of King Philip to whom 'they would deliver the whole kingdom'. To encourage Essex, O Neill, on behalf of the Spanish King, promised him great favours and, as Essex expressed some doubts because of 'certain disservices he had done to the Crown of Spain', O Neill went so far as to offer him his son as a hostage in proof of his good faith.

In *The Great O Neill,* p. 220, Ó Faoláin quotes a translation of this letter from Mateo de Oviedo and it is interesting to note that the misinterpretation of a single word causes him to dismiss the account as 'obviously a fabrication of Tyrone'. The word occurs in the sentence in which the Archbishop refers to O Neill's offer of his son as a hostage to Essex: 'Onel le *daba* en rreenes a su hijo', the translation of which is 'O Neill *was giving* him his son as a hostage', and not 'O Neill *gave* him his son . . .' as assumed by Ó Faoláin. Of course O Neill did not give his son to Essex; according to Mateo's letter, he had not succeeded in persuading the English Viceroy, consequently the question of a hostage would have become irrelevant. When Mateo wrote his letter from Donegal, Essex, banished from the court, was under house arrest awaiting trial. His execution did not take place until ten months later, in February 1601.

In Spain, the news of O Donnell's death was the cause of grief and desolation among the Irish. From La Coruña, Caracena wrote to the King:

> *The news of the Earl Odonel's death has been received here and I mourn his loss deeply for many reasons. All the Irish people here are extremely grieved and afflicted and they believe that the death of the Earl puts an end to their hopes of help and to the hopes of all the catholics of that kingdom.*

Caracena urged the King to send letters to O Neill so that his supporters be not discouraged on hearing of O Donnell's death, and the King ordered that money, arms and munitions be sent to Ireland, but his orders were not carried out for several months.

Meanwhile, O Neill continued to evade his enemies while making overtures of peace to Mountjoy and, from Glanconcadhain, on Christmas eve 1602, he dispatched a messenger with letters for King Philip and for the

Archduke Albert, governor of Spanish Flanders, explaining his position, asking that the promised aid be sent promptly and that, if it could not be sent to arrive before 1 May of the following year, a ship be dispatched to carry him and his few remaining associates away from 'the fury of their enemies'.

Throughout the year which followed the defeat of Kinsale, Queen Elizabeth had consistently refused to allow any negotiations with O Neill; as late as October 1602 she wrote to Mountjoy: 'Wee still remaine determined not to give him grace in any kinde.'   It was not until February 1603 that, as Mountjoy wrote to Sir Robert Cecil, the Queen's Secretary of State, he received from the Queen: 'a letter wherein it pleased her to enlarge the authority given unto me to assure him of his life, liberty and pardon upon some conditions remembred therein . . .'   It has been suggested that approaching death softened the Queen's heart, but it is more likely that her change of mind was due to fear of O Neill's escape to Spain and of the powerful influence a man of his prestige, remarkable genius and qualities of leadership would have, were he allowed to make personal contact with King Philip and his ministers. This fear is expressed in many letters of English government officials and in particular in a letter of November 10th, 1602, from Mountjoy and his Council to the lords of the English Privy Council:

> *When we foresee how dangerously he is compounded to do mischief if he escape cutting off and should work himself into the favours and means of Spain, we are bold in discharge of our duty to propose to your lordships as a matter very considerable in this conspiring time whether it be not better to have him stayed for a time upon some temperate conditions than if he should get away .*

O Neill shrewdly played on this fear in his letters to Mountjoy asking him to negotiate his peace with Queen Elizabeth and suggesting, in a letter of December 1602 that he might be: '. . . driven into utter despair either to fly or to seek any other Prince . . .'   and again in March 1603: '. . . that I be not cast into an utter despair to forsake my native country . . .'

The letters which O Neill had written from Glanconcadhain on Christmas eve 1602 to King Philip and to the Archduke Albert reached Brussels in April 1603 after a long delay of three months.   By then, having received no answer, O Neill had been forced to come to terms with Mountjoy, and the death of the Queen of England in March 1603 brought about a new phase in Hispano-English relations. Many in England, however, could not believe that the enemy who had so long and successfully waged war against them was now beaten and a Spanish agent reported from London:

> *A great number of people believe that Tyrone's submission is a feint in order to gain time and to improve his position .'*

During the summer of 1603, Hugh O Neill, Earl of Tyrone, and Ruairí O Donnell, younger brother of Red Hugh, and soon to become Earl of Tyrconnell, travelled to London to give obedience to James I who had succeeded Elizabeth on the English throne. While in England, they wrote secretly to Philip III saying that, if the peace which was then being negotiated between Spain and England were not obtained, they would immediately rally to the service of the Spanish King and take up arms against the King of England. Moreover, as the Earls reminded King Philip some years later:

> *Although the eleven years' war came to an end at that time, nevertheless we were not discouraged from continuing in Your Majesty's service and, as soon as we had come to terms with the enemy, we sent Mac William Burke with a message to Your Majesty in the year 1603, informing you of what had happened, begging you to send us help and declaring that we would continue in your royal service with the same good will and loyalty as always. During the following year we sent several messages to the Conde de Villamediana, Your Majesty's ambassador in London, offering to be of service to Your Majesty if the peace negotiations with England were not successful; and one of us went in person to speak of this matter secretly with the ambassador .*

However, terms of peace were agreed upon by Spanish and English representatives and, in London in August 1604, a treaty was signed by which, among other stipulations, neither of the monarchs was to give countenance to the rebellious subjects of the other. This of course referred particularly to English help against Spanish rule in the Low Countries and Spanish help to the Irish.

James I had restored O Neill and O Donnell to most of their lands and O Donnell had been created Earl of Tyrconnell but, judging by many subsequent complaints and memorials of the Earls, it is evident that the English King's ministers in Ireland were intent upon dismantling the estates of Tyrone and Tyrconnell and removing all traces of the traditional Irish laws and customs which had upheld the power and influence of the Earls. On 4 July 1605, King James issued a proclamation denying the Irish catholics their liberty of conscience, forbidding them the private use of their religion, ordering all catholic priests to leave the country before the 10th of the following December and requiring their flocks to attend protestant churches under pain of fines and imprisonment. The catholics of the Pale and of the cities were not exempt from these laws despite the fact that many of them had opposed O Neill during the war against Queen Elizabeth. They protested strongly, but to no avail, and some of them were arrested and imprisoned. During the following year of 1606, according to the account of O Neill and O Donnell, representatives of these catholics of the cities and of the Pale had secret meetings with the Earls and pledged themselves to take up arms when help from Spain would arrive. In Dublin, government ministers had some suspicion of the existence of this league of Irish catholics or, as they termed it, this conspiracy. Certain disclosures by Christopher St Lawrence, Baron of Howth, were the cause of some anxiety to the new Lord Deputy, Sir Arthur Chichester. He sent a report on the matter to London and, in July 1607, he received a reply in the following terms from the lords of King James' Privy Council:

> *Although the discourses of the priests, the brags of the Irish at home and abroad of the good entertainment from the Spaniards, with the assurances of the Irish both of town and country, now especially weary of English government for matters of religion, are enough to prove ill-intention on all sides . . . yet all these things are not worthy to draw on the King to any sudden action. Because first it might alarm the Irish, especially those he has tampered with and force them into rebellion .*

In the meantime, Ruairí O Donnell had paid a secret visit to the Spanish ambassador in London; his journey to England was unlikely to have aroused suspicion because his wife, Bridget Fitzgerald, daughter of the 12th Earl of Kildare, was closely related to the influential Howard family in England. Bridget's mother was Frances, daughter of Charles Howard, Earl of Nottingham, Lord High Admiral and member of the English Privy Council, and Frances was then employed at court as governess of King James' daughter, the princess Elizabeth. O Donnell travelled to London towards the end of 1604 and, one night in December of that year, with the utmost secrecy, he made his way to the Spanish embassy to deliver to the Conde de Villamediana the message which O Neill and himself had agreed upon. The import of the message was that, if King Philip felt that the peace with England was unlikely to last, the Earls and their confederates were ready to wait for a period of up to two years, even in the difficult circumstances in which they found themselves, for the possible renewal of hostilities with England, when they would be ready to act in Ireland on Philip's orders. However, if he was convinced that peace was firmly established, they asked that a ship be sent to take them wherever the King might wish, while awaiting to see how affairs developed, for they said they could no longer live in safety in their country and they feared the power of the English King who had inherited, along with the kingdom of Queen Elizabeth, the hatred which she bore them. Finally they reminded the King of his obligation to them and asked for financial aid.

Undoubtedly, the measures taken by James' ministers in Ireland, designed to diminish the estates and the power of the Earls, were having a corresponding effect on their income and adding to their difficulties, particularly in regard to their attempts to circumvent their enemies' designs for, as they pointed out some months later, they had not the means 'of bribing the heretics so as to gain them over'.

King Philip's answer, following the recommendation of his Council, was that he did not wish to endanger the peace with England and that the treaty would now make it possible for him to intercede with the King of England on behalf of the Irish. However, the appeal for financial aid did not go unheeded and, despite some delay caused by the death of the King's confessor, Don Gaspar de Córdoba, who had been entrusted with the matter, there are records of large sums ordered to be paid secretly to O Neill and O Donnell. It is interesting to note that, at the same time, Philip III was paying pensions to six members of King James' Privy Council, including the chief Secretary of State, Sir Robert Cecil, Earl of Salisbury, and the lord Treasurer, Thomas Sackville, Earl of Dorset. The others were the Viceroy of Ireland, Mountjoy, who had been created Earl of Devonshire on his return to England, and three members of the Howard family, the Earls of Northampton, Suffolk and Nottingham. Northampton was a brother of the Duke of Norfolk who was accused of treasonable conspiracy with Mary Queen of Scots and was executed in 1572; Suffolk was the Duke's son, and their kinsman, Nottingham, was Lord High Admiral of England. The purpose of their pensions is explained in a memorandum of the Conde de Villamediana:

> When we had concluded the negotiations for peace between His Majesty and the King of England, the Condestable de Castilla and I had a consultation regarding the persons whom it would be advisable to put under obligation by giving them annual pensions in money or jewellery, at their choice, so that they might attend willingly to matters concerning His Majesty's service in this kingdom, as was His Majesty's intention.

The ambassador also advised the King that these members of the English Privy Council wished their pensions to run as from the date of the signature of the peace treaty and to be paid 'always through the intermediary of those ladies', presumably their wives, 'so that they themselves might be free of what could be imputed to them'. The Earl of Devonshire accepted a pension of £750 and the others were to be given £1,000 each but, on the advice of Villamediana, Salisbury's pension was raised to £1,500; using the code name *Beltenebros* by which Salisbury is designated in most of Villamediana's reports, the ambassador explained his reason thus:

> This Beltenebros is so haughty and proud that I believe he will consider a pension of one thousand pounds to be a paltry sum and undoubtedly he will resent receiving the same amount as the others.

Robert Cecil, Earl of Salisbury, was the son of Lord Burghley, Queen Elizabeth's long-serving secretary of state; Cecil had succeeded to that position on his father's death in 1598 and, on King James' accession to the throne in 1603, he was continued in his post. He had the misfortune of being a hunchback, but this in no way prevented him from gaining enormous influence over the King who called him his 'little beagle' and created him Viscount Cranbourne in 1603 and Earl of Salisbury in 1605. Despite the fact that he accepted a Spanish pension, Philip's ambassadors found him most uncooperative and difficult to deal with. He is reported to have said to the Earl of Northampton in the latter's apartments at Hampton Court:

> *Mylord, all that is needed to draw me to the service of the King of Spain (provided it would involve nothing against my King or against my reputation) would be that we should find means whereby I should not lose the honour which my father and myself have gained by persuading the people that we were absolute enemies of Spain and by causing them to conceive hatred for that country. If I were to depart from this long-held attitude, I would be looked upon as a traitor and could then achieve nothing either for myself or for those of the persuasion of the Spanish ambassador.*

His sympathies inclined towards the Dutch enemies of Spain from whom, it was suspected, he also received a substantial pension. Despite the fact that a later ambassador of Spain considered Cecil 'not worth any expense whatever', he continued to receive his pension until his death in 1612 for, as King Philip's ministers pointed out, the purpose of these pensions was 'to encourage some to do good and to prevent others from doing harm'.

In March 1605 Ruairí O Donnell, Earl of Tyrconnell, was again in London where he had further interviews with the Spanish ambassador. Villamediana took the opportunity of consulting him on various matters concerning the Irish, of which King Philip had written to him, including the suggested appointment of O Neill's son, Henry, as colonel of the Irish in the Spanish army of Flanders. Henry, or Don Enrique as he was known in Spain, was then eighteen years of age and was at the court in Valladolid. The ambassador's report of O Donnell's opinion on that point is as follows:

> *As regards sending Don Enrique Onell to Flanders, it does not appear suitable that he should be employed so close to England in the service of the Catholic Majesty; this would give offence to the King of England, for the Earl of Tiron, father of Don Enrique, and the Earl of Tirconel, his uncle, are slaves of the English King until such a time as the Catholic Majesty may be inspired by God to undertake their deliverance from this slavery .*

However, other considerations prevailed with King Philip and, later that year, Henry O Neill was appointed to serve in Flanders as colonel of an Irish regiment which was to remain in existence until the last years of that century, and was always commanded by an O Neill. To distinguish it from other Irish regiments formed subsequently in the Spanish service, it was known eventually as the 'Old Irish Regiment', *el Tercio Viejo Irlandés*, and because of the fact that six successive Earls of Tyrone were an colonels, it was also known as the Regiment of Tyrone. The formation of this regiment in 1605 was a means of giving employment to many of the Irish who had sought refuge in Spain since the disaster of Kinsale and the end of the war; perhaps also its particular usefulness in the event of renewed war with England was a consideration which led the King to authorise its formation under Colonel Henry.

Undoubtedly, diplomatic relations with England were strained and many contemporary reports show that O Neill would have been justified in thinking, as he appears to have done, that the peace would not last. Various incidents provoked angry reactions and on both sides claims were made that neither the letter nor the spirit of the peace treaty was being observed. At the outset much indignation was caused at the English court by the fact that King James' title of King of Ireland had been omitted from the Spanish ambassador's letters of credence. Continuing acts of piracy were complained of to the English ambassador in Spain as well as to his counterpart in London. On numerous occasions the Spanish ambassador protested to King James and his ministers that English pirates were allowed to attack and rob Spanish ships and that these offences were condoned by the authorities, which was contrary to the terms of the treaty. The King and Salisbury countered these accusations by claiming that English merchants had been ill-treated in Spain and that their cargoes had been confiscated and, moreover, that King Philip gave shelter to Irish rebels and to those who conspired against the life of King James, in whose mind the gunpowder plot of November 1605 still loomed large.

One of the more serious diplomatic incidents at this time involved an Irishman named Juan Wall. In 1604 Wall was chosen as secretary and interpreter to accompany the Condestable de Castilla, chief of the Spanish commissioners appointed for the peace negotiations in London. After the signing of the treaty he returned to Spain with the Condestable and when, the following year, Don Pedro de Zúñiga was appointed to replace the Conde de Villamediana as ambassador in London, Wall was ordered to travel with him to England to serve again as secretary and interpreter. It was not long before Don Pedro was told that King James' ministers would not dare to converse with him through the intermediary of an Irishman and that his presence had not pleased the King. Thereafter, the ambassador used the services of another interpreter, but Salisbury resorted to the extraordinary measure of ordering Wall's arrest within the Spanish embassy.

In a lengthy letter of 18 July 1606 to Philip III, the ambassador reported the events of the previous day. At 11 o'clock in the morning a note from Salisbury was delivered to him requesting that he secure the person of his secretary Juan Wall who was accused of conspiring to kill King James. Don Pedro describes the long and stormy interview he had in the afternoon with the King and with the councillors; finally, at 10 o'clock that evening, the secretary of the Privy Council was sent to arrest Wall and to remove him from the embassy. Don Pedro considered hiding Wall or using force to oppose his arrest, but he decided against this, believing, as he wrote, that it would be used as an admission of guilt. However, he declared to those who came to arrest Wall that, though he could not prevent them from doing so, it was done against his will and he was convinced that his secretary was innocent of any crime. In fact nothing was ever proved against him and, though he was kept in prison for over a year, he was eventually released and he returned to Spanish Flanders.

The circumstances which provided the excuse for Wall's arrest were that he had recently returned from Brussels, where he had been sent with letters from the ambassador, in the company of Captain Thomas Francesqui. Francesqui and Wall would have been well acquainted for both had served for several years in the Spanish army of Flanders in the regiment of Sir William Stanley.

Stanley was an English catholic who, under Queen Elizabeth, had recruited an Irish regiment to serve the Dutch allies of England against Spanish Flanders. In 1587 he surrendered the Dutch town of Deventer and, with his troops, joined the opposing Spanish army. After the signing of the Anglo-Spanish peace treaty, King James sought the extradition of Stanley and of his one-time lieutenant-colonel, Jacques Francesqui, a brother of Captain Thomas, alleging that they were implicated in plots against him; Stanley was regarded in England as a traitor and it was known that Guy Fawkes had served with his regiment in the Spanish army of Flanders, but the Archduke Albert held out against the demands of the King of England.

Within a week of Thomas Francesqui's arrival in London in the company of Wall, he also was arrested on a charge of conspiracy to kill the King. In concluding his long report of these events, the Spanish ambassador wrote:

> *The King was very insistent on having him* [Wall] *removed from my house, for he says that the Colonel* [Jacques Francesqui] *poisoned an accomplice* [of the gunpowder plot, presumably], *who could have revealed the names of the others. All this I hold to be a deceit and it is my belief that they wish to take revenge in any possible way on Colonel Francesqui who, they say, has spoken very freely to their ambassador* [in Brussels] *against the King and, what is worse, against the Earl of Salzberi, which in this kingdom is a crime of lese-majesty.*

In Spain, it was not long before King Philip's ministers formed the opinion that the English were deliberately testing Spanish reactions. Their recommendation to the King was that, if he wished to have peace, he must prepare for war and, with regard to the Irish regiment, they added:

> *letters should be sent to the Archduke and to the Marques Spinola asking them to have particular care to give the best treatment in every way to Don*

Enrique O Neill and to the men of his regiment, and to procure that their numbers be increased to the greatest possible extent, for if the peace with England be broken, it will be of great importance to have the good will and devotion of the Irish. It will also be of great importance to have many experienced soldiers of that nation so that we may send them to start a war in Ireland where the English fear it so much, for experience has shown that the war in Ireland was, for the English, what the war in Flanders was for Spain.

From England it was reported that the lord high admiral, Earl of Nottingham, had counselled merchant friends of his to withdraw their property from Spain for it was his belief that the peace would not last three months. At the same time the French ambassador in London wrote to Paris:

It is my opinion that the English and the Spaniards are so dissimilar in all things except in their excessive pride, as regards which I know not who holds the advantage, that without any encouragement from us it cannot be long before we see them come to grips again.

It was then two years since the signature of the peace treaty but the situation had become so tense and feelings were running so high that war appeared inevitable.

CHAPTER TWO

The Escape of the Earls

In Ireland in the meantime, English officials were succeeding gradually in dispossessing O Neill of much of his lands and his sources of income. On his return from London in August 1603, he found that King James' letters patent, granting the restoration of the greater part of his estates, were no guarantee either against the encroaching policies of the Dublin government or against the designs of unscrupulous officials.

The English lawyer, Sir John Davies, was appointed Solicitor-General for Ireland in November 1603 and Attorney-General in May 1606, and took seriously his duty of extending the application of English law to what he termed 'the Irishry in the Province of Ulster . . . the most rude and unreformed part of Ireland, and the seat and nest of the last great rebellion.' Like most Englishmen of his day, Davies considered the Irish and their way of life to be barbarous and uncivilised; this view strengthened him in his purpose which was 'that the next generation will in tongue and heart and every way else become English; so as there will be no difference or distinction, but the Irish Sea betwixt us . . . For heretofore, the neglect of the Law, made the English degenerate, and become Irish; and now, on the other side, the execution of the Law, doth make the Irish grow civil and become English.'

Born in 1569, Davies attended Oxford, was admitted to the Middle Temple in 1588, and was called to the bar in 1595. He has been described as 'a versatile, gifted, renaissance Englishman' who was 'at once lawyer, jurisprudent, poet, antiquarian and statesman.' Undoubtedly he had many talents; however, he had other attributes which did not endear him to some of his contemporaries. He was disbarred in 1597 for breaking a cudgel over a fellow barrister's head while in hall, and the circumstances surrounding this incident suggest vindictiveness on the part of Davies rather than a hasty temper. The object of his anger, one Richard Martin, had made fun of Davies who, in planning his revenge, made sure of being accompanied by two swordsmen and of having a boat ready on the river at the Temple steps by which to make his escape. Re-admitted to the bar in 1601, he found favour with Queen Elizabeth, and also with King James, both of whom admired his poetry. In Ireland, he proved to be a relentless adversary of O Neill whom he regarded as the greatest obstacle to the anglicisation of Ulster. Also, he resented the fact that, as a defeated enemy, the Earl of Tyrone had been allowed to retain so much of his lands and that he was still looked upon by his people with the traditional respect accorded to the 'sacred name of their O Neale.' Consequently Davies directed his efforts towards reducing 'the greatness of this Earl.'

O Neill, on his part was much incensed by the arrogant manner of Davies and considered him to be 'a man more fit to be a stage-player than a counsel" to King James, an observation which is not out of keeping with some contemporary accounts of the man.

When the viceroy Mountjoy returned to England in the summer of 1603 he left, as his deputy, the Treasurer Sir George Carey. In February 1605 this appointment was transferred to the governor of Carrickfergus, Sir Arthur Chichester, who for the following ten years worked in close co-operation with his Attorney-General, Sir John Davies. Some six years older than Davies, Chichester in his youth is said to have fled to Ireland to escape arrest because he had 'robbed one of Queen Elizabeth's purveyors, who were but little better than robbers themselves.' Having obtained the Queen's pardon, he served in the English navy against the Spanish Armada of 1588; he was a volunteer in the expedition to Cádiz under Essex in 1596 and, some two years later, he was sent to Ireland in command of a regiment of 1,200 men. He was appointed governor of Carrickfergus in succession to his brother who had been killed in action in 1597, and he became privy councillor in the Dublin government in April 1603.

In March 1605, within a month of Chichester's instalment as deputy viceroy, O Neill wrote to the Secretary of State in England complaining of many wrongs done to him for which he could get no redress from the King's ministers in Ireland. Three months later he wrote that attempts were being made to take away from him his hereditary rights over the fishing of the river Bann and of Lough Foyle. In December 1605 he appealed to the King to clarify the meaning of his patent so as to put a stop to the many claims being put forward against him for, he wrote:

> *I have been before the now Lord Deputy's time many ways troubled by such as since the time of the granting of my patents have scanned very nearly thereupon and have pried so nearly into it that, unless Your Majesty will vouchsafe by expounding your royal meaning and exposition of my patent, the courses lately held against me will grow to the overthrow of my whole estate.*

He received no answer from King James and, in February 1606, O Neill and O Donnell instructed their representative in Spain to present a memorial to the Spanish King explaining the increasingly difficult circumstances to which the English King's ministers had reduced them and reminding King Philip of his promise of financial aid, which had not yet taken effect:

> *From the Earl Onel they have taken five lordships, some of which were of sixty and fifty miles and the least in extent was of thirty miles, and from the Earl*

*Odonel they took almost as much. Apart from this, they have left on the lands of
the Earls many garrisons which are still there, maintained at the expense of the
Earls and preying on the Earls' poor vassals. So that, because they have served
Your Majesty, the Earls have lost lives, estates and wealth and are reduced to
their present state of miserable servitude, in danger at every moment of losing
their own lives and constantly receiving from those ministers offences and
injuries to their consciences, their honour and their possessions . . . The Earls
have sent the petitioner to represent to Your Majesty their extreme necessity and
to say that, because they have not the means of maintaining their houses, nor of
bribing the heretics so as to gain them over, they are forced and resolved to escape
with their lives and to seek Your Majesty's protection, if Your Majesty does not
send them financial aid by some secret means, without causing scandal in
England and without endangering the lives of the Earls .*

The man who presented this memorial on behalf of O Neill and O
Donnell was Matha óg Ó Maoltuile; he had served the Earls well and
faithfully for many years and was later to be instrumental in bringing to
Lough Swilly the ship in which they made their escape in September 1607.
In the English State Papers his name appears under various guises:
Matthew Tully, Matthew O Multally, Matthew Flood, Matthew Oge,
Mack Oge, Mag Ogy. In Spain he was known as Mateo Tulio. He had
joined the Spanish navy in 1591 and, some few years later, returned to
Ireland to serve in the war. In 1602 he was in Spain with Red Hugh O
Donnell and acted as his secretary. After O Donnell's death at Simancas he
returned to Ireland by order of King Philip, probably with messages for O
Neill. In 1604 he carried letters from Ruairí O Donnell to the English
Secretary of State, Sir Robert Cecil, with complaints against King James'
ministers in Ireland; at the same time he was entrusted by O Neill and O
Donnell with secret messages for the newly appointed Spanish ambassador in England. In London, in December of that year, he acted as
interpreter between O'Donnell and the ambassador, Conde de Villamediana. Matthew Tully himself states that, shortly afterwards, he was
forced to leave Ireland and return to Spain because, when his past services
became known to the English, they sent express orders to the said Earls O
Neill and O Donnell to dispense with his services and to banish him from
their lands and their company. For that reason he was forced to leave
Ireland and all his property and to escape to Spain to save his life.

While King Philip and his councillors were considering the memorial
which Matthew had presented and deliberating upon the amount of
money to be sent to Ireland and the manner of sending it, O Neill appealed
again to King James and, from Dungannon, on 17 June 1606, he repeated
his request that his letters patent be clarified for, he explained, many were
taking advantage of the patent's lack of precision to lay claim to much of
his estate and, he added:

the chief ground of such as seek to take my living from me riseth upon colour of terming divers parcels of my inheritance to be monasteries, priories and abbey lands, and that the Bishops of Derry and Clogher, where their predecessors had only chief rent, would now have the land itself; I most humbly beseech Your Highness to stop any such mean courses, and that they may be contented with that which their predecessors have formerly enjoyed these many years past.

O Neill's repeated requests eventually appeared to have some effect for, on 2nd September 1606, the Lords of the Privy Council in London wrote to the Lord Deputy Chichester instructing him to take:

more than ordinary care to free him [the Earl of Tyrone] *and protect him from any unnecessary molestation upon any ordinary process or information of any troublesome persons because it is a matter subject to charge and disgrace from both which, as long as he shall remain obedient to the state, his Majesty would have him freed.*

Chichester, however, was hardly the man to ensure that the Earl did not suffer 'unnecessary molestation'. He had seen much active service against O Neill during the later years of the war in Ireland, in the course of which his brother had been killed. At the conclusion of the war, he had been disappointed in his hope of gaining substantially from the expected confiscation of O Neill's lands which adjoined the estates he had acquired in north-eastern Ulster for, even more than his predecessor, Mountjoy, Chichester was given to 'greedy gathering'.

The Attorney-General, on his part, had perceived the advantages to be gained from the loose wording of O Neill's letters patent. In November 1606 he wrote to the Earl of Salisbury, King James' Secretary of State, arguing that much of what O Neill claimed as hereditary right was, in his opinion, 'a mere usurpation and a wrong' and that many of his possessions, having been vested in the crown in the reign of Queen Elizabeth, 'they do, notwithstanding the Earl's patent, remain in the Crown still; and consequently all O Cahan's country and all the freeholders' possessions in Tyrone are actually and really in His Majesty's hands,' and so free to be disposed of at the will of the King and his Council.

At this time, it was judged by O Neill's adversaries that King James' friendly attitude towards him was an obstacle to their aims of, on the one hand, the anglicisation of Ulster, and on the other, the acquisition of the possessions of a defeated enemy. Early in 1607, a friend of O Neill's at the English court, Sir Patrick Murray, a Scottish gentleman of the King's household, sent him warning that accusations were being made against him to the King and, in particular, that he had been accused of abusing his authority of martial law, in other words, that he was no longer 'obedient to the state'. The Earl found it necessary once again to write to King James:

I am given to understand that Your Majesty have been informed that I should (by martial law) execute someone that hath done good service unto the late Queen of famous memory, whereat Your Highness seemed to have conceived some dislike. My dread Sovereign, may it please you to be advertised I have not executed any one man by martial law sithence Your Highness coming to the Crown of England but that I made good account of, as well before the Lord Deputy and Council here as also before the Lords Justices of Assizes in their circuit from time to time, which was of them very well accepted and allowed for good service, so as I thought little there should ever grow any more speech thereof. But now that Your Majesty have been informed thereof by whosoever, my humble suit unto Your Highness is that the informers be brought either before Your Highness there, or Your Majesty's Deputy here to justify their accusations, whereby Your Majesty may be satisfied at full and the suggestion to be proved to the contrary, Your Majesty may perceive me to be wronged by some that would be privy adversaries unto me, and by these and like suggestions seek to bring me in Your Majesty's disfavour and to work my overthrow .

The matter was pursued no further, but the seeds of suspicion had been planted in the mind of the King. Around this time, both the French and the Spanish ambassadors in London reported that King James' ministers had found they could lead him whatever way they wished by reminding him of the possibility of further plots against his life. Indeed, he had been so scared by the various plots which had already come to light, particularly the Guy Fawkes attempt, that he wore thick layers of padding quilted into his doublets to render them stiletto proof.

O Neill's difficulties were then added to by the claims of his son-in-law and sub-chief, Donal O Cahan, whose lands traditionally had formed part of O Neill territory. After the defeat of Kinsale and the death of Red Hugh O Donnell, O Cahan had offered his services to Chichester against O Neill. Whatever the reason for his betrayal, his defection could not have come at a worse time for O Neill and for those who were still in arms. After the war, despite his services to the Crown, he was refused his request to have his lands detached from the O Neill lordship. He now renewed his efforts in that direction and, following the long-standing policy of 'fanning dissensions' among Irish chieftains, the resultant dispute was encouraged by Chichester and Davies. A new arrival, the King's Bishop of Derry, added fuel to the fire. George Montgomery, rector of a parish in Somersetshire, was appointed bishop of the united sees of Derry, Raphoe and Clogher in 1605. On May 20th of that year, his wife, Susan, wrote to inform her brother of the news:

My Lord Bishop [her husband]*will be at home before Wednesday night. The King hath bestowed on him three Irish bishoprics; the names of them I cannot remember, they are so strange, except one, which is Derry: I pray God it may make us all merry .*

It was not until October of the following year that the Bishop and his wife took up residence in Derry. On 8 October 1606 the Bishop's lady wrote to her brother:

We are settled in the Derry, in a very pretty little house builded after the English fashion . . . I think that Mr. Montgomery will not set any of his lands before that time [the following spring] he hath many thousand acres of as good land as any in England; if it were peopled, it were worth many hundred pounds by the years .

Bishop Montgomery's views with regard to the chieftains of the north were naturally in accordance with those of the Dublin government. O Cahan's dispute with his father-in-law had generated a legal wrangle in the course of which he was used as an instrument by the government in an attempt to weaken the power of O Neill, and by Chichester and Montgomery in the hope of increasing the extent of their estates. In March 1607 the continuing dispute led to a confrontation between O Neill and Davies who declared to the Earl: 'I rest assured in my own conceit, that I shall live to see Ulster the best reformed province in this kingdom; and as for yourself, my lord, I hope to live to see you the best reformed subject in Ireland.' To this, O Neill replied that he hoped from his heart the Attorney-General might never live to see the day when injustice should be done him by transferring his lands to the Crown, and thence to the bishop who was intent on converting the whole territory into his own pocket. Shortly afterwards, on 26 May 1607, O Neill wrote to King James from Mellifont:

Whereas it pleased Your Highness of your great bounty to restore me by letters patent to such lands as I and others my ancestors had and enjoyed in her late Majesty and others, Your Highness' predecessors' times excepting Sir Henry Oge O Neill, knight, his country, and Sir Turlagh Mc Henry O Neill, knight, his country, passed unto them by letters patent, as also certain other parcels of lands reserved to Your Highness for occasions of service, by reason whereof my living and revenue is much lessened, yet was I well satisfied with the rest (such being Your Majesty's pleasure) but now, most gracious Sovereign, there are so many that seek to despoil me of the greatest part of the residue which Your Majesty was pleased I should hold, as without Your Highness' special consideration of me I shall in the end have nothing to support my estate, for the Lord Bishop of the Derrye, not contented with the great living Your Majesty has been pleased to bestow on him, seeketh not only to have from me unto him a great part of my lands, whereunto none of his predecessors ever made claim, but also setteth on others (as I am informed) to call into question that which never heretofore was doubted to be mine and my ancestors. Your Majesty's Counsel at

Law likewise under pretence of Your Majesty's title doth call the chief substance of the rest of my living in question, namely, these parcels, Killitragh, Glanconkene, Slieveshiese, Slugh Arte and Traghticahan, for that they are not specially named in my letters patent, whereas, in truth, there is not one parcel particularly named in them, and by like reason they may take from me all the lands I hold, except I may be protected and upholden herein by Your Majesty, upon whose grace and favour I must wholly depend. I most humbly therefore beseech Your Highness that you would be pleased to direct your gracious letters to the Lord Deputy here, thereby commanding him to make new letters patent to me and my heirs.

O Neill also complained to the King that Bishop Montgomery had incited O Cahan to repudiate his wife, O Neill's daughter. The Bishop denied O Neill's charge that he had stirred up O Cahan against him. However, he made the following admission in a letter to Salisbury on 1 July 1607:

I did not think fit to dissuade him [O Cahan] *nor deem it amiss to ease myself of the labour of the trial with the Earl which otherwise I must have undertaken* [in order to claim as church land part of O Neill's territory] *but was contented to make use of this occasion offered into my hand and to encourage O Cahan in his intended course . . . It was thought fit in policy of State to separate O Doghertie from O Donel . . . O Cahan is of greater power to offend or benefit in respect of the vicinity and largeness of his country and is thought (under correction) no less needful to be freed from the Earl.*

When Ruairí O Donnell had been received to favour by King James in 1603, the lands of the O Donnell lordship which the royal grant restored to him did not include those of his sub-chief, O Dogherty. The Bishop cited this as a precedent for the case of O Cahan.

It was now no longer merely a dispute between O Neill and O Cahan; the case had become a trial of strength between the Earl and the ministers of King James. Eventually it was decided that the case would be heard in England and, on 16 July 1607, the King wrote to Chichester, ordering that both parties present themselves in London at the beginning of the following Michaelmas term and requesting also the presence of the Attorney-General to act as his adviser.   It would appear that by then O Neill's enemies had succeeded so well against him that, on arrival in London, he would have been accused of treason, committed to the Tower and executed, for such was the warning O Neill and O Donnell declared they received from 'intimate friends of theirs on the King's very Council.' These friends are not mentioned by name in any of O Neill's letters to Spain, but there are indications which suggest the identity of at least one of them. At the court of King James there were those who, though outwardly conforming with the establishment, would have preferred to see a catholic monarch on the English throne. The correspondence of the Spanish

ambassador, Conde de Villamediana, and of his successor, Don Pedro de
Zúñiga, reveals that among this group they had particular friends and
informants to whom they referred as *los confidentes* and three of whom are
mentioned regularly under their code names of *el Cid, Roldan* and *Malgesi*.
However, in one unguarded report, the identity of *el Cid* is disclosed: he
was Henry Howard, Earl of Northampton,   and was considered by King
Philip's ambassadors to be Spain's most reliable friend in the English
government; he was a member of the Privy Council and, privately, he was
a catholic. It is possible, therefore, that he was one of those responsible for
the warning sent to the Earls of Tyrone and Tyrconnell.

Northampton was a brother of the Duke of Norfolk who was
executed in 1572 for treasonable conspiracy with Mary Queen of Scots.
Northampton himself was implicated in the conspiracy and suffered several terms of imprisonment. Nevertheless, he was re-admitted to court in
1600, James I made him privy councillor in January 1604 and, later that
year, he acted on the commission appointed to negotiate terms of peace
with Spain. He was considered to be the leader of the 'Spanish faction' at
the English court and was opposed to the policies and the aggressive
attitude towards Spain of the Earl of Salisbury and his followers. In a letter
of August 1606 the Spanish ambassador gives an interesting glimpse at the
intrigues of the English court:

> *The ministers who dislike him* [the Earl of Salisbury] *are the greater number and
> the most powerful: Malgesi* [?], *el Cid* [Northampton], *Luster* [Leicester?], *the
> Admiral* [Charles Howard, Earl of Nottingham], *the Treasurer* [the Earl of
> Dorset], *and Gerosberi* [the Earl of Shrewsbury] *who, having married his
> daughter to the Earl of Arundel* [Thomas Howard], *is considered as belonging to
> the House of Howard, Oton* [Hatton?] *who is devoted to the Howards and is a
> supporter of the peace treaty, and the Baron Guillermo* [Sir William Howard,
> brother of the Earl of Suffolk], *a great catholic gentleman of whom I wrote to
> Your Majesty. They are considering forming a league against Beltenebros*
> [Salisbury] *if he does not comply, within reason, with their wishes.*

Against this background of intrigue, it is naturally among the members of the 'Spanish faction' that we must look for O Neill's 'intimate
friends on the King's very Council'; it would have been to the advantage of
catholics, not only in Ireland, but also in England and Scotland, that O
Neill should remain free and active. As yet I have found no clue to the
identity of *Roldan* and *Malgesi;* however, the fact that the Spanish ambassador had such a well-placed informant as Northampton adds strength to
his statement to King Philip, written shortly after the 'flight of the Earls':

> *I know that they wish to kill him* [O Neill] *by poison or by any possible
> means* .

The French ambassador in London, who had his own informants at the English court, expressed similar views in a report to Paris and suggested that the dispute over land ownership between O Neill and O Cahan had been instigated by English officials so that King James might have an obvious reason for summoning him to London because, according to his report:

> it was feared that if he [O Neill] were ordered to come, he might suspect the aim in view, which was to put him in the Tower and, moreover, not to let him linger there long .

According to O Neill's letters to Spain after his escape from Ireland, he believed that King James knew nothing of the league of Irish catholics which had been formed over a year earlier, but he was mistaken. In the early summer of 1607, the Earl of Salisbury in London and the Lord Deputy, Chichester, in Dublin, were alerted to the existence of the league by an informer who declared that there was 'a general revolt intended by many of the nobility and principal persons of this land, together with the cities and towns of the greatest strength; and that they will shake off the yoke of the English government, as they term it, and adhere to the Spaniard.'

The informer was the Baron of Howth, Christopher St Lawrence, who, tradition tells us, was once kidnapped by the pirate queen Grace O Malley because she had been refused hospitality by the young Christopher's grandfather at Howth Castle. The unusual terms of ransom, to which Lord Howth agreed, were that henceforth the gates of the castle should never be closed against anyone seeking hospitality, and that an extra place should always be laid at his table.

During O Neill's war, Christopher St Lawrence served with the English forces under Essex, whom he accompanied on his unauthorised journey to England, and for whose sake he offered to kill Lord Grey de Wilton and Sir Robert Cecil, later created Earl of Salisbury. On his return to Ireland, St Lawrence served under Mountjoy and, some time after the end of the war, disappointed in his expectations of reward, he sought service in Spanish Flanders where he remained for several months and where, according to the reports of English spies, he was on friendly terms with the son of the Earl of Tyrone, Colonel Henry O Neill. Early in the summer of 1607 he returned to London and to Dublin to disclose what information he had obtained first to the Earl of Salisbury and later to Chichester.

Among those whom St. Lawrence implicated in the planned insurrection were Ruairí O Donnell, Earl of Tyrconnell, and Richard Nugent, Baron of Delvin. As for the Earl of Tyrone, Chichester reported to Salisbury that the informer 'was unable to charge him with any particular matter but was well assured by the speech he had with the former two and with others, in the Low Countries, that he is as deep in the treason as any.'

This was not the first time that Chichester had sought to elicit information which he might use to O Neill's detriment; Cuchonnacht Maguire, chieftain of Fermanagh and staunch supporter of the Earl of Tyrone, had been arrested and held for questioning by the Lord Deputy who, as O Neill claimed, was 'very desirous and earnest to aggravate and search out matters against him [O Neill] . . . and specially and very distinctly examined M'Gouire and used many persuasions to him to signify if he might lay any matters to his charge.'   Maguire gave nothing away but towards the end of May 1607 he left Ireland for Flanders and, three months later, he was one of those involved in organising the escape of the Earls of Tyrone and Tyrconnell.

A comparison between St Lawrence's disclosures and O Neill's account of the plans of the secret league of Irish catholics shows some points of similarity and many discrepancies. It would seem, therefore, that St Lawrence had drawn on his imagination to add to the information he had obtained. O Neill's account confirms that the league existed, that it included many of the principal persons of the cities and towns, and that they planned to take over certain strongholds when help from Spain would arrive. But the Baron of Howth's account goes further and claims that the King of Spain had been approached and had promised aid of men, money and munitions, whereas it is clear from O Neill's memorials to King Philip that no direct appeal had been made to the King on behalf of the league before the 'flight of the Earls'. 'Up to the present', the Earls wrote from Louvain to King Philip in December 1607, 'there was no occasion to inform Your Majesty of the matter.'

What St Lawrence stated concerning Fr Florence Conry is of particular interest in view of Fr Conry's close association with and constant support of O Neill and O Donnell. St Lawrence declared that in the Low Countries 'he met with one Flarie Omulconnor, known by the name of Father Florence provincial of the Irish Franciscan friars, by whom he was assured that all things were concluded, and that himself was to go into Ireland to ascertain the lords, cities and towns of the aid promised and to conclude with them for the time . . . and that Father Florence had received, by direction from the King [of Spain], five or six thousand pounds for his use.'

After the death of Red Hugh O Donnell in September 1602, Father Conry had remained at the Spanish court urging the King to send help to O Neill. In April 1603 he accompanied Don Martín de la Cerda who sailed from La Coruña with two ships carrying arms, supplies and money to O Neill by order of King Philip. But it was too late; in the words of a memorial referring to that journey: 'He found that the Earl and the other catholics (being at the end of their resources) had come to terms with the enemy and, so as not to draw suspicion upon them, he did not disembark and he returned to Spain.'   MacWilliam Burke joined Father Conry's ship at Achill and returned with him, bringing messages from O Neill for King Philip. In April 1604, in order to deal more effectively with the great number of refugees from Ireland, a member of the Spanish Council of State was named Protector of the Irish; he was Don Francisco Arias Dávila, Conde de Puñonrostro, and Father Conry was appointed as his adviser. In May 1606, at the General Chapter of Toledo, he was elected Provincial of his order; he then sought and obtained permission to return to Ireland to exercise the duties of his office, and he was granted five hundred ducats, the equivalent of two hundred and twelve pounds sterling in values of the time, for the expenses of the journey and the purchase of necessary equipment. At his request, King Philip also authorised the foundation of an Irish Franciscan College at Louvain, with a yearly grant of two thousand ducats for its maintenance.

Florence Conry left Madrid in February 1607 accompanied by, among others, Matthew Tully, the envoy of O Neill and O Donnell at the court of Spain. They travelled first to Spanish Flanders where, at Louvain, Father Conry was detained for some months occupied with the foundation of the Franciscan College of St Anthony. St Lawrence's meeting with Father Conry in the Low Countries could have taken place during the first few months of 1607, but it is most unlikely that, as he reported, the Franciscan Provincial told him that the King of Spain would aid the Irish 'with 10,000 foot and 200 horse at the first, and supply them as there should be occasion.'

It is true, however, that Father Conry planned to return to Ireland. A letter from King Philip, dated 11 August 1607, orders that he be paid in Flanders three hundred crowns, the equivalent at that time of one hundred and fifteen pounds sterling, to enable him to continue his journey to Ireland; the sum of five or six thousand pounds mentioned by St. Lawrence in this connection is clearly an exaggeration.

In Dublin, Chichester was alarmed at the extent of the plot uncovered to him by St Lawrence, yet he doubted the trustworthiness of the informer whom he had earlier described as 'unstaid'. St Lawrence consistently refused to be named as the discoverer of the plot and insisted that no third party should be present when he spoke of it to Chichester. From Dublin Castle in July 1607, the Deputy wrote to Salisbury: 'I wish I had the assistance and company of a third person when I speak with him, for I like not the business especially to deal with him alone therein, for the end may be so full of hazard as that the work will require more labour. I recommend this to Your Lordship's consideration and do humbly pray from time to time to be instructed and directed by your letters for my carriage therein.'

The Secretary, however, appeared not to take the matter very seriously and, on 22 July 1607, a letter was dispatched to Chichester from Salisbury and the lords of the Privy Council assuring him that it was 'not worthy to draw on the King to any sudden action; because first it might alarm the Irish, especially those he has tampered with and force them into rebellion.' They also point out that it would have been advisable for Chichester to have 'rectified a little the strong discontent of the towns and others now boiling in their hearts . . . Their loyalty would then be confirmed and the less would be their jealousy if there were occasion to lay hold of any persons of rank.'

It is interesting to note that only a few days earlier King James had written to Chichester ordering that O Neill and O Cahan present themselves in London at the beginning of the following Michaelmas term, that is, in late September or early October. Apparently, Salisbury's main concern was to ensure that O Neill should obey the summons unsuspectingly so that, once in London and away from his own people, he could be dealt with summarily; as the Earls were to declare later:

> *When they* [King James' ministers] *considered that we are the principal leaders of the catholics and that, if they captured us in England, they would have little to fear in Ireland despite all persecutions, the King of England summoned us to London with the intention of either beheading us, or putting us in the Tower of London for life.*

The warning which was sent by O Neill's friends of the English Privy Council reached him probably at about the same time as the summons from King James, for Chichester remarked afterwards: 'It is observed here by some that knew him best, that since he received His Majesty's letter for his repair thither, he did lose his former cheerfulness and grew often exceeding pensive.'

The message cannot have come as a surprise to the Earls, for events had been moving towards some such crisis and already in February of the previous year they claimed in a memorial to King Philip that they were 'in danger every moment of losing their lives.' O Neill does not tell us how and by whom the warning was conveyed to him; the only indications available are to be found in the unreliable statements of various people who were arrested and questioned by Chichester after the Earls' escape. Of these, the most plausible account is given by the Franciscan Father Thomas Fitzgerald who was questioned at Dublin Castle on 3 October 1607 [*old style*]. According to his statement, shortly after the 'flight', he was sent by his superior, the vice-provincial Father Owen Groome Magrath, to the Earl of Tyrconnell's wife at Maynooth, 'to assist her until he brought her to her husband', but these plans miscarried and he was arrested. With regard to the circumstances of the Earls' departure, the record of Father Fitzgerald's statement gives the following details:

> *He* [Father Fitzgerald] *saith, further, that Owem Groome Magrath told him that the Earls of Tyrone and Tyrconnel had sent one John Bath into Spain, five or six months since, to pray the King of Spain's favour and assistance, they*

being fearful to be taken or sent for into England, from whence and the Low Countries they received several answers and intelligences soon after, one of which was by a priest named Rory Albanagh, another by an officer of one of the Irish company's, either an ensign or a serjeant, whose name he knoweth not, nor of what company he was.

Rory Albanagh came about midsummer last, and the officer not a month before their departure. Rory told him that the King of Spain would have them rather to go into England than come unto him, for he would give no offence to the King, our master, by receiving them, being in league with him; but, said he, the King and the Archduke will write to the King, their master, to be gracious unto them if they had offended. But soon after this it was informed out of England to their friends in Flanders, especially to the Archduke, that the Earl of Tyrone was sent for into England, and that he should never return back into Ireland again, and that the Earl of Tyrconnel should be taken and committed in Ireland: whereupon the ensign or serjeant above said was sent to acquaint them on that side, willing them withal to be in readiness to attend the coming of a ship, which should be sent for them soon after; and having delivered this message, he returned, as Rory Albanagh had done before.

The said Owen told him further that the ship was a Frenchman, and that she came out of Brittany; that she was met withal and stayed a day or two by a Scottishman betwixt the lands of Ireland and Scotland, and being released, she came and anchored at Lough Swilly about the 25th of August [old style, i.e. 4 Sept. new style], and gave out that she was come to the fishing, having good store of salt and nets aboard; she remained there nine days. John Bath was master; and in her came over Cuconnaught Maguire, Matthew Tully, and Donough O Brien.

Upon their first coming to Lough Swilly, this Donough O Brien landed by night, and went to the Earl of Tyrconnel to acquaint him with the arrival of the ship; whereupon Tyrconnel sent notice thereof to Tyrone by the above said Owen Groome Magrath.

Letters they brought none from the King of Spain, Archduke or Pope; but they brought in money the sum of 1,500 pounds to bear their charges.

The said Owen told the examinate further that Donough O Brien told him that the Earls were sent for to preserve them from danger, and that they should remain beyond seas upon the King's charge; but they should not be admitted to the court until there should be a conclusion to the treaty in hand betwixt the King of Spain, the Archduke, and the Hollanders.

Owen Magrath said further, that if the peace be not agreed on and concluded betwixt the King of Spain and the States, and that if the King, our master, take part with the Hollanders, then will the Spaniard break the peace with England, and send an army this next spring into Ireland; otherwise, if the peace be concluded, the King of Spain will continue and confirm the league with England and persuade the King to pardon their offences, and to settle them in their countries in the same state that they were before the last rebellion, with

*liberty of conscience at least in their own countries. And if there were war, the
Pope had promised to assist them with 50,000 crowns yearly, and with some
men, if he could conveniently bring it to pass . . .*

*He saith he expected the coming over of Father Florence this last summer,
who is the provincial of his order, and this Owen Groome Magrath is his deputy
in Ireland; but now he thinks he will not come until there be some settlement or
alteration.*

Except for the Pope's reported promise of 50,000 crowns yearly,
Father Fitzgerald's statements are not out of keeping with the information
uncovered in Spanish archives.

John Bath, or Rath, of Drogheda, the captain of the ship which took
the Earls to safety, had already served as O Neill's messenger to Spain in
1599 ; it is not unlikely that he would have acted again in the same
capacity.

King Philip's views, which Father Fitzgerald claimed were reported by
Rory Albanagh, are consistent with his answer to the Earls conveyed to
them two years earlier by the Spanish ambassador in London,   and with
his attitude towards the Earls after their escape. Of course much of what
passed between O Neill's representatives in Spain and King Philip and his
ministers would not have been recorded. In this connection it is interesting
to note that Matthew Tully, O Neill's officially accredited representative
in Spain, was at the Spanish court, as King Philip stated, 'attending to
certain matters relating to my service';   this was in September 1606, and
his departure for Flanders was delayed until about the end of January 1607,
when he travelled to the Low Countries with Father Florence Conry. We
do not know what were these matters relating to the King's service which
delayed Matthew's journey, but what little evidence there is would suggest that they were in some way connected with O Neill and his plans.

The warning sent to the Earls from England is described by Father
Fitzgerald more or less as it is in their memorials to King Philip.

The names of those who brought to Lough Swilly the ship by which
the Earls made their escape, are confirmed in later memorials and in the
account of Tadhg Ó Cianáin,   the chronicler who sailed with them, and
also in the reports of English spies. Cuchonnaught Maguire and his
companions were well suited to their task. Maguire is described by the
Four Masters as a 'rapid-marching, adventurous man, endowed with
wisdom and beauty of person.'   It was also said of him that he was able to
disguise himself so that his nearest friends would have found it difficult to
identify him.   As far as is known, his only experience of life on the
continent amounted to the two months he had spent in the Low Countries
since his arrival there about the end of May 1607; but, if such was the case,
he could rely on the knowledge of his fellow travellers. Matthew Tully had
spent many years in France and Spain, knew the languages well, and had

been stationed for some time with the Spanish army in Brittany. Donagh O Brien, or Dionisio as he was called in Spain, also had experience of life on the continent. He himself tells us that, as a child, he spent a long time in exile, though he does not specify in what countries. He returned to Ireland to serve in the war and, in June 1602, he went to Spain in the ship which, by order of King Philip, had brought supplies to O Sullivan Beare and the chieftains of Munster. Back in Ireland after the end of the war, he was offered large rewards by Sir Oliver Lambert, President of Connaught, if he would accuse the Earl of Tyrconnell of treason; he refused to do so and managed to escape to Flanders. As for John Rath, he was an experienced sea captain with many voyages to his credit.

The negotiations for peace in the Low Countries were of particular relevance to the Irish who must have followed their progress with anxious interest. It was well known that, despite the Anglo-Spanish peace treaty of 1604, England continued unobtrusively to help the Dutch provinces in their war against Spain. A break-down in Hispano-Dutch negotiations might encourage King Philip similarly to help the Irish against England, and O Neill and his supporters would have awaited and welcomed such an opportunity. In the Low Countries, after many years of war and varying fortunes, the campaigns of 1605 and 1606, though costly, had been successful for the Spanish army under their commander-in-chief, Ambrosio Spínola, against Maurice of Nassau and the army of the Dutch provinces. During the following winter, feelers for peace were put out and the result was a truce of eight months signed in May 1607 by the Archduke, governor of Flanders, and acknowledging that Spain had no claim over the United Provinces of Holland. Three months later, King Philip ratified the truce, unwisely signing the document 'Yo el Rey' as he was accustomed to do within his dominions. Many troubles and difficulties arose and prolonged the negotiations, to which all the powers of Europe sent ambassadors. It was not until April 1609 that the Twelve Years Truce was finally agreed and signed. It would be quite understandable, therefore, that in 1607 King Philip should not have wished to add to the difficulties of the negotiations by receiving O Neill at his court.

As regards Father Florence, Owen Magrath's opinion proved correct; he did not return to Ireland and, at this time, his change of plans must certainly have been connected with the imminent escape of the Earls. In view of the support he gave to the northern chieftains during the war, he was probably in their confidence and must have known their intentions. He was described by the contemporary Archbishop of Armagh, Peter Lombard, as being 'more eager to sustain the war than the very officers of the army itself.'

News of O Neill's summons to London would have reached the court of the Archduke in Flanders about the beginning of August 1607. According to the English ambassador at Brussels, Sir Thomas Edmonds, Cuchonnaught Maguire then went to Brittany and there, 'disguising himself as a merchant bought some wines and salts and hired a ship at Nantes, wherein he landed his merchandises, together with a provision of fishing nets, to give colour to his going to fish upon the coast of Ireland.'

He brought the ship to Dunkirk and, from that port, sailed with his companions to Ireland.

O Neill's movements in the days prior to his escape on 14 September 1607 may be traced in the narrative of Tadhg Ó Cianáin who takes up his account eight days before the event. News of the arrival of the ship in Lough Swilly reached O Neill by a message delivered to him on September 6th. He was then at Slane, apparently to meet Chichester with whom he had several interviews and who described the visits thus: 'The Earl of Tyrone came to me there oftentimes upon sundry artificial occasions, as now it appears, and, by all his discourses, seemed to intend nothing more than the preparation for his journey into England against the time appointed.' Two days later, O Neill left Slane and spent the night of the 8th at Mellifont in the house of Sir Garret Moore. The lands and buildings of Mellifont Abbey were granted to Edward Moore, Sir Garret's father, in 1566 and remained the seat of his family until the eighteenth century. Sir Garret gave help to Red Hugh O Donnell at the time of his escape from Dublin Castle in 1592 and, although he served with the Queen's army against O Neill during the war, he appears to have remained on friendly terms with the northern chieftains. He served as intermediary between O Neill and Mountjoy in 1603 when O Neill sued for terms of peace and it was at Mellifont in March of that year that the treaty was finalised.

According to Chichester: 'The Earl of Tyrone often made use of Sir Garret Moore's house in most of his passages between Dublin and his country and at sundry other times.' In fact, O Neill had placed his son, John, to be educated with the family of Sir Garret. John, born in October 1599, was the eldest of O Neill's three young sons by his fourth wife, Catherine Magennis, and, when the Earl left Mellifont on the afternoon of Sunday 9th of September, he took the boy away with him. On the following morning, Sir Garret reported his departure to Chichester, who sent one of his captains after O Neill 'to see what he did.' Some time later, the Deputy wrote to Salisbury:

> The manner of his departure, carrying his little son with him who was brought up in Sir Garret's house, made me suspect he had mischief in his head; harm I knew he could do none, if they were upon their keeping, for he was altogether without arms and munition; and his flight beyond the seas I should never have suspected, but I thought by posting after him, I should in a short time understand more of his purposes. The first news I heard was of his departure which, in my opinion, is far better for the King and Commonwealth than if he were in the Tower of London.

On leaving Mellifont, O Neill travelled through Dundalk, Silverbridge, Armagh and Dungannon, and on Monday 10th of September he reached 'the Craobh, one of his island habitations' in the vicinity of Stewartstown, where he remained for two nights and a full day. It is possible that his wife, his youngest son Brian, then about three years of age, and other members of his household were there at that time and it may be that this deviation from his direct route to Lough Swilly was for the purpose of collecting them and bringing them with him. Ó Cianáin gives no indication of this but, if we are to believe the report of Sir John Davies, who omits to mention the source of his information, O Neill was accompanied by his wife from Wednesday 12th:

> *On Wednesday night, they say, he travelled all night with his impedi-*
> *ments, I mean his women and children; and it is likewise reported that the*
> *Countess, his wife, being exceeding weary, slipped down from her horse, and,*
> *weeping, said she could go no further; whereupon the Earl drew his sword, and*
> *swore a great oath that he would kill her in the place, if she would not pass on*
> *with him, and put on a more cheerful countenance withal.*

The Countess Catherine would have had good cause for being exceeding weary, because on that day, Ó Cianáin tells us, O Neill's journey had brought him across the Sperrin mountains. At midday on the 13th, they arrived at Ballindrait, the home of the Earl of Tyrconnell's younger brother, Cathbharr O Donnell. There, the group rested from midday to nightfall, when they continued their journey, accompanied by Cathbharr O Donnell and probably also his wife and other members of his household. Cathbharr was married to Róis O Dogherty who, after his death which was to occur in Rome the following year, became the wife of Eoghan Rua O Neill. They crossed the river Foyle some five miles below Strabane and, at daybreak on Friday 14th, they reached Rathmelton. The last eight miles of their journey lay along the shore of Lough Swilly to Rathmullen where, Ó Cianáin records, their ship was at anchor and where 'they found Ruairí O Donnell, Earl of Tyrconnell, and the aforesaid gentlemen *(Maguire, O Brien, Tully and Rath]* together with many of the tribe and followers of the Earl, putting stores of food and drink into the ship.'

Among them was Nuala O Donnell, sister of Ruairí and Cathbharr, who had left her husband, Niall Garbh O Donnell, when he deserted her brothers' cause and offered his services to the English. Ruairí's wife, Bridget Fitzgerald, was at Maynooth, left to grieve that force of circumstances prevented her from being with her husband, but their little son Hugh, not yet a year old, was there with his nurses. From Rathmullen, according to Sir John Davies, they sent for the two-year-old son of Cathbharr and Róis, also named Hugh, who was at fosterage. O Neill's five-year-old son, Conn, was at fosterage also, but could not be found; concerning this boy Chichester wrote to the Privy Council in London:

> *I have given warrant likewise to Sir Tobias Caulfield to make search for*

Con O Neill, one of the Earl's children, among his fosterers in Tyrone, and to take him into safe custody, until he receive other direction in his behalf. This child was by accident left behind, for the Earl sought him diligently, but by reason he was overtaken with shortness of time, and that the people of those parts do follow their creates, as they call them, in solitary places, and where they best like their pastures (after the manner of the Tartars), they are not, therefore, always ready to be found.

Several attempts were made afterwards to rescue the child and take him to Flanders, but to no avail, and Conn was not among the ninety-nine who, Ó Cianáin tells us, went on board the ship at Rathmullen and set sail at about midday on Friday 14th of September 1607. In a memorial to King Philip, the Earls themselves give a brief but evocative description of their escape:

They hurried to a sea port of their country and, leaving their horses on the shore with no one to hold their bridles, they went aboard a ship to the number of about one hundred persons, including soldiers, women and principal gentlemen.

The news of the Earls' escape caused consternation at the court of King James, where it was assumed immediately that they had gone to Spain. At this time, a report of the Spanish ambassador in London describes the state of panic which the news had provoked in that city, and may be taken as a measure of the reputation which O Neill had gained. On 3 October the ambassador wrote to King Philip:

A member of the Council of Ireland   has come with the news that the Earl of Tiron, his children, the Earl O Donel and other Irish gentlemen have gone to Spain. This has caused such commotion here that they believe that the fleet, which set sail some days ago on Your Majesty's orders, is going to Ireland under Tiron's command. The King was quite distraught at the news . . . The following Sunday all the members of the Council met in London and . . . a great multitude of people waited thinking that the peace would end on that day . . . and now they are saying that Tiron will start a war on behalf of the Pope with the encouragement of Your Majesty.

The ambassador's report goes on to show that Salisbury handled the situation with an impressive show of calm and control. However, the letter which he wrote on that subject to the English ambassador in Madrid, Sir Charles Cornwallis, would suggest that he was not as unconcerned as he wished to appear. From Hampton Court on 27 September 1607 [*old style*], Salisbury wrote to Cornwallis:

Concerning those men that are fled into Spain, His Majesty hath commanded me to give you some directions how you are to proceed. . . Because His Majesty would not have you set a value upon their worth, by making their flight any matter of consequence to any other body but to themselves, he would have you proceed in this sort.

First, upon this letter, which toucheth the matter of injustice to the King's subjects, you shall do well to make your access; and when you shall have therein spent the best part of your audience, if the King shall say nothing to you of those men, then His Majesty would have you obiter, *even as if you scarce had it in premeditation, say to the King, that although you have not now anything in particular to propound unto him concerning those Irish fugitives by any new commission, yet because His Majesty, in a later despatch, even in the postscript of a letter only, spake something shortly of it, you cannot forbear the rather upon this occasion to say something to His Majesty of it, by virtue of your general commission . . .*

For the words of the King's letter, you may say they were to none other effect than this: that his deputy of Ireland had advertised him that some of the northern Earls, and some others out of those barbarous quarters of Ulster, were gone into Spain; of whose proceedings, though he held the parties too contemptible to make any reckoning . . . yet you do hope that will minister to His Majesty there so excellent a subject to requite the King your master's sincerity with demonstration of his integrity in his proceedings towards them . . .

Because you may not apprehend this matter worse than there is cause, nor make any show of alteration — what insolencies soever the Jesuits and pack of fugitives do there put on — I do confidently affirm it unto you, that in human judgment the end thereof cannot but be good. For although it is true that we do know this remnant of the northern Irish traitors to have been as full of malice as flesh and blood could be, and noway reformed by the grace they have received, but rather sucking poison out of the honey thereof; yet because His Majesty had given them pardon, and could not demonstrably prove new treasons against them so clearly in foro judicii, *as they might have not suspected to savour of rigour, yet,* in foro conscientiae, *His Majesty hath known they have absolutely given commission to their priests and others to undertake for them a resolution to abandon their sovereign if they might be entertained, not sticking to avow their alienation of heart from the English government . . .*

If the Council of Spain shall conceive that they have now some great advantage over this state . . . there may be this answer: that those Irish, without the King of Spain, are poor worms upon earth; and that when the King of Spain shall think it time to begin with Ireland, the King, my master, is more like than ever Queen Elizabeth was to find a wholesomer place of the King of Spain's where he would be loathe to hear of the English, and to show the Spaniards that shall be sent into Ireland as fair a way as they were taught before. In which time, the more you speak of the base, insulting, discoursing fugitives, the more proper it will be for you.

The Earl of Tyrone's brother, Cormac O Neill, remained in Ireland probably by arrangement with the Earl, whose intention was to return the head of an army and lead the planned insurrection. Cormac w married to Margaret O Donnell, a sister of the Earl of Tyrconnell, and two of their sons, Brian and Art óg accompanied the Earls. When the ship had sailed, Cormac went to Dublin to bring the news to Chichester and to petition for a *custodiam* or wardenship of his brother's estates. But the Deputy regarded him with suspicion and noted that he had waited a full day before bringing the news to Dublin. He was arrested and imprisoned in Dublin Castle; three months later, in December 1607, he was sent to the Tower of London where he ended his days. Another son of his, Brian Crosach O Neill, was accused of conspiracy and hanged in Derry in 1615. Brian's mother, Margaret O Donnell, in fear for the safety of her youngest son, ten-year-old Conn, who was being sought by the authorities, succeeded in getting him away to Flanders. She joined him there herself in 1622.

CHAPTER THREE

The Earls in Flanders

When the Earls sailed away from Lough Swilly, they intended to go to La Coruña in north-western Spain, and on to the court at Madrid to put forward their case in person to King Philip; but they were driven off course by storms and contrary winds and, after a perilous journey of twenty days, they finally reached land on 4 October 1607 at Quillebeuf, near Le Havre in France. They were particularly unlucky; given fair wind and weather, they could have reached La Coruña in four or five days, but Ó Cianáin tells us that, when they had rounded the coast of Donegal and drawn level with Croagh Patrick:

> Then they feared that the King's fleet, which was in the harbour of Galway, would meet with them. They proceeded out into the sea to make for Spain straight forward if they could. After that they were on the sea for thirteen days with excessive storm and dangerous bad weather. A cross of gold which O Neill had, and which contained a portion of the Cross of the Crucifixion and many other relics, being put by them in the sea trailing after the ship, gave them great relief. At the end of that time, much to their surprise, they met in the middle of the sea two small hawks, merlins, which alighted on the ship. The hawks were caught and were fed afterwards. On Sunday, the 30th of September, the wind came right straight against the ship. The sailors, since they could not go to Spain, undertook to reach the harbour of Croisic in Brittany at the end of two days and nights. The lords who were in the ship, in consequence of the smallness of their food-supply, and especially of their drink, and also because of all the hardship and sickness of the sea they had received up to that, gave it as their advice that it was right for them to make straight ahead towards France.

At that point, they may have been in the Bay of Biscay, for they told the Archduke, governor of Flanders, that they had come within eight leagues of La Coruña. At any rate, they landed at Quillebeuf at the mouth of the river Seine on 4 October and, on the following day, the women and children were put on a boat to travel up river as far as Rouen. But the Earls and their group were delayed, for although the governor of the town had shown them every kindness and had entertained O Neill to dinner on the day after their arrival, in return for which O Neill presented him with the hawks they had caught at sea, yet he would not allow them to continue their journey until he had received permission from the King of

France to whom he had reported their arrival. Despite the efforts of the English ambassador in Paris, Sir George Carew, to have the Earls arrested and sent to England, King Henry IV of France, while denying them their request for permission to travel to Spain, allowed them to pass freely through northern France to the Spanish territory of Flanders. Ó Cianáin tells us that, when the Earls were prevented from continuing their journey,

> *Matha Ó Maeltuile went post-haste to Paris. The governor's messenger reached the King of France sooner than Matha and got a reply. He returned. The King was returning from hunting when Matha went into his presence. He spoke face to face with him. He told him all the adventures of the lords, how they were prohibited to traverse the kingdom of France until they should have the King's authority. The King said respectfully and kindly that he had received letters concerning the gentlemen before that, and that he had written to the governor about them. Matha went to the King's secretary. He said that no harm at all would come to the princes because of their detention, and that a friendly answer from the King would reach them sooner than Matha would have returned.*

In London, Salisbury had been informed of the Earls' arrival in France and of King Henry's attitude towards them. He wrote to Sir Thomas Edmonds, the English ambassador in Brussels:

> *More certain information has been received that they being weatherbeaten at sea, are put in at Kilboeuf in Normandy, and at their landing obtained leave of the Duke of Montpensier* [the marshal of Normandy] *for their safe passage towards Brussels, with all their retinue. Whereof Sir George Carew being advertised, addressed himself to the French King and provisionally desired him to make stay of them so long there till he might receive further order out of England in that behalf; which request he the rather grounded upon the French King's speeches proceeding from his own mouth at his last audience, which was but a few days before, when the French King thought they had been landed in Spain, 'that the King of Spain did wrong to His Majesty to receive them.' Notwithstanding he now made him a quite contrary answer: that France was a free country for passengers and that, the Duke of Montpensier having already given his word for their safety, the King could not revoke it.*

Nevertheless, it is clear from Ó Cianáin's account that the Earls and their followers did not feel safe from their enemies' attempts until they should have reached the territories of the King of Spain:

> *When Matha óg* [Ó Maeltuile] *came to Rouen, and when he learned that the order and direction they received was to go to Flanders, he himself went post-haste to Flanders to tell O Neill's son, the Colonel of the Irish in Flanders under the power of the King of Spain, that these lords came from Ireland, that they had trouble and lost their way on sea, that they came to land in the kingdom of France, that they were hindered so that they were not allowed to take the short*

journey to Spain, that they were obliged to make straight for Flanders, that they were asking the colonel to come to meet them to the border of France, and also to procure for them a passport and warrant from the Archduke the same as the warrant of the King of France to the border of his kingdom . . . On the next day, the fifteenth of October, they left Rouen with thirty-one on horseback, two coaches, three waggons, and about forty on foot. The governor of Quilleboeuf and many of the gentry of the town came to conduct them a distance from the city.

On 18 October they crossed the French frontier and reached the town of Arras, then within the borders of Flanders, where the Bishop of Clogher, Eoghan MacMahon, had come from Douai to meet them. They arrived at Douai on the 22nd and visited the Irish College where they were met by Father Florence Conry and Father Robert Chamberlain, both of whom had been so active on their behalf. They remained in that town for three days and, no doubt, O Neill discussed his plans with his two Franciscan friends and perhaps it was on their advice that a few days later, from the town of Tournai, he wrote to the Papal Nuncio at Brussels, Archbishop Bentivoglio, describing the circumstances of his escape from Ireland.

On 31 October, at Halle, some fifteen kilometres south of Brussels, the Earls were met by O Neill's son, Henry, whom they had not seen for over seven years and who was now twenty years of age, a graduate of Salamanca University and Colonel of the Irish Regiment in the Spanish army of Flanders. Still at Halle, on 3 November, they were visited by the Marqués Ambrosio Spínola, commander-in-chief of the army and secretary of finance in the government of Flanders, and on the 5th they travelled to the court at Binche where they were received by the Archduke Albert and his wife the Infanta Isabel who greeted them at the entrance of their palace and brought them to their private appartments. Two days later, they were entertained to a banquet given in their honour by the Marqués Spínola at his palace in Brussels; they were given a military escort into the town and, when they reached their destination, the Marqués himself, the Papal Nuncio, the Spanish ambassador and the Duke of Osuna came to take them from their coaches. Ó Cianáin describes the scene for us:

When greetings had been exchanged in abundance, they entered the hall of the Marquis and spent some time in conversation. Afterwards they entered the apartment where the Marquis was accustomed to take food. He himself arranged each one in his place, seating Ó Néill in his own place at the head of the table, the Papal Nuncio to his right, the Earl of Tyrconnell to his left, Ó Néill's children and Maguidhir next the Earl and the Spanish ambassador and the Duke of Aumale on the other side, below the Nuncio. The rest of the illustrious, respected nobles at table, the Marquis himself, and the Duke of

Osuna were at the end of the table opposite Ó Néill. The excellent dinner which
they partook of was grand and costly enough for a king, and nothing inferior was
the banquet. Gold and silver plate was displayed inside that no king or prince in
Christendom might be ashamed to have. They spent some time in conversation
and chatting, and they took leave and returned thanks to one another.

To O Neill's European contemporaries, the long war of the Irish
chieftains against the forces of Queen Elizabeth would have appeared as
the struggle of a David against the superior strength of a Goliath. Because
of his successes in the earlier years of the war, O Neill had achieved
remarkable fame, and it was no exaggeration on his part when he declared:
'The events of this war were known throughout Europe for we gained
many victories, and caused the loss of much enemy infantry and artillery
and of the flower of England's nobility and militia.'

In those days of uncompromising religious attitudes, O Neill was
called a traitor and an 'archfiend' by his adversaries of the reformed
religion, but in catholic countries of Europe he was looked upon as a
champion of the faith and he was treated accordingly. The King of France
allowed the Earls and their followers free passage through his country. At
Douai, in various colleges of the University, they were presented with
addresses at assemblies held in their honour. At Tournai, the governor
came to meet them outside the walls of the town, cannons were fired in
salute as they entered, and coaches were made available for their use. At
Nivelles, the keys of the town were offered by the governor to O Neill. At
Binche and at Brussels, their reception by the Archduke and the Infanta,
and by their ministers, was such as might be accorded to the visiting
princes of a friendly state.

Certainly, such a reception was not in keeping with the expectations
of Sir John Davies who, in a letter to Salisbury, had expressed the opinion
that O Neill and his 'train of barbarous men, women and children . . . will
be taken for a company of gypsies and be exceedingly scorned'.   As
regards O Neill himself, Davies wrote: 'when the formal Spanish courtier
shall note his heavy aspect and blunt behaviour . . . they will hardly believe
he is the same O Neill which maintained so long a war against the crown of
England.' In contrast, it is interesting to note that Don Francisco Ruiz de
Castro, Conde de Castro and Duke of Taurisano, who was Spanish
ambassador in Rome for many years and who knew O Neill well, wrote of
him to King Philip: 'The Earl is a great nobleman and Your Majesty owes
much to his loyalty and devotion.'   As for Ruairí O Donnell, Earl of
Tyrconnell, Davies had remarked: 'He will appear to be so vain a person,
as they will scarce give him means to live, if the Earl of Tyrone do not
countenance and maintain him.'   But this was not the opinion of Don
Juan de Tassis, Conde de Villamediana, Spanish ambassador in London,

who had several interviews with O Donnell, concerning whom he wrote to King Philip: 'The man made a very good impression on me.'

When the formalities of their arrival at the court of the Archduke were over, O Neill and O Donnell were anxious to be on their way to Spain to carry out their intention of explaining to King Philip the plans of the league of catholics in Ireland and the reasons for which they believed a rising would be successful, given the minimum of help from Spain. They stayed in Louvain for a week, preparing for their journey, and they probably spent long hours discussing the political situation and their chances of gaining support from Spain. The negotiations for peace between Spanish Flanders and the United Provinces of Holland were then at a critical stage. A temporary truce declared in April 1607 was due to end in December and already the Archduke had named the members of the commission who were to travel to the Hague to renew discussions with the Dutch in January 1608. They included the Marqués Spínola and the Franciscan Commissary General Fr Juan Noyen. At that time there seemed little hope that agreement would be reached. It was an unstable situation and, from the Irish point of view, despite the Anglo-Spanish peace treaty, it was reasonable to hope that Spain would wish to back a rising in Ireland; O Neill would have been impatient to get a hearing from King Philip or, more realistically, from the Duke of Lerma. If he did not already know the circumstances of the Spanish court and the Duke's influence over the King, certainly he would have received a thorough briefing from Father Conry and Father Chamberlain.

For obvious reasons, the Earls decided to leave a number of their followers in Flanders, including the ladies and the children. Having made arrangements for their families at Louvain and for those who would remain behind with them, O Neill, O Donnell and Maguire set out from that city on 25 November 1607 with their retinue, thirty horsemen in all. Their intention was to travel first to Rome and there to seek the Pope's blessing and support for their plans, then to proceed to Genoa and take ship for Spain.

On 8 November the Archduke had written to King Philip describing the good reception he had given to the Earls and to those who accompanied them; he informed the King of the Earls' intention of continuing their journey to Spain, and enclosed a list of the names of those who would be travelling with them. A letter of the same date from the Marqués Spínola informed the King that a sum of 12,000 crowns had been given to the Earls, 5,000 each to O Neill and O Donnell and 2,000 to the Countess of Tyrone. Spínola's letter mentioned also the complaints of the English ambassador at Brussels, Sir Thomas Edmonds, to the Archduke regarding the good reception accorded to the Irish: 'The ambassador of England asked His Highness to order that the Earls be arrested and sent to their King. The answer which His Highness sent was that his country was free to all, and that there was no way in which he could accede to that request, all the more as he knew not that the Earls had done anything to deserve it.'

Philip himself had already received strong representations on the same subject from James' representative in Madrid and, on November 11th, yielding to pressure or, as he put it, 'to avoid causing offence or suspicion to the King of Great Britain', he had sent orders to his ambassador at Brussels, the Marqués de Guadaleste, instructing him to get from the Earls a written account of their plans and their intentions, on consideration of which he would make his decision known to them; meanwhile they were to remain in Flanders. However, letters between Madrid and Brussels seldom took less, and often more, than three weeks to reach their destination. When Guadaleste received these instructions from the King, the Earls had already set out on their journey. The ambassador's reply, written from Brussels on 4 December 1607, provides an interesting sidelight on this episode:

> When I received Your Majesty's letter of the 11th of November, the Earls Honel and Odonel had already left for Spain by way of Italy. I sent a letter after them, asking that, before continuing their journey, they should send to me the Father Provincial, Fray Florencio Conrio, who accompanied them as interpreter and counsellor. They did so, and remained at Namur. I told the Friar of the orders which Your Majesty had sent me in your royal letter. He was grieved at this, although I gave him the message in the best possible manner. He returned and, on the following day, Colonel Don Henrique, the son of the Conde Onel, came and told me they had decided to return to Louvain and, from there, they would send me in writing the reason for their coming and what they intended to ask Your Majesty.
>
> I reported all this to His Highness, who answered me that this was satisfactory but that they should not remain in these states, for their presence here would give rise to the same objections as if they were in Spain. I begged His Highness to delay telling them this until receipt of Your Majesty's reply, but it was not possible for him to grant me this favour because of the promise he had made to the English ambassador. And so, by order of His Highness, the Marques Espinola has taken the responsibility of telling the Earls that, knowing they had resolved to go to Spain, His Highness gave his word to the ambassador of England that within very few days they would leave these states and, as the ambassador is pressing His Highness to keep his promise, the Marques is to try to persuade the Earls to go to Milan or to Rome and there, to await Your Majesty's decision.
>
> I do not know how the Earls will take this and I confess to Your Majesty that it seems to me His Highness has taken a harsh decision on this matter with regard to people who have given such service to God and to Your Majesty, as will be seen in their letter to Your Majesty, whom I humbly beg to show them the favour they deserve.

At this moment, I have just been given the Earls' letter and, as this dispatch will be taken by Pillasco, who is a servant of the Marques Espinola, it is not sent in code.

In the letter of the Earls to King Philip, they explain the difficult situation of catholics in Ireland since the end of the war against England in 1603; they describe the formation of a secret league with plans for a new rising against English domination; they declare that, during the previous year and a half, attempts had been made on their lives on secret orders from ministers of King James and that they had received warning from friends of theirs in England that, when the King had summoned them to London, it was with the intention of beheading them or of putting them in the Tower of London for life; they appeal to King Philip for help with which they would return to Ireland to lead the planned rising and they point out the benefits which would ensue, not only for the catholics of Ireland, Scotland and England, but also for the monarchy of Spain, if the King would accede to their request for help and would accept their offer of bringing Ireland under the crown of Spain, and they conclude as follows:

We call God to witness that, if Your Majesty does not accept this offer of ours made on behalf of the whole kingdom, and no kingdom ever made offer more willingly, as we shall prove by shedding our blood and giving our lives in the service of Your Majesty, you will be called to account for it before the supreme judge. Moreover, the catholics of those three kingdoms, who have placed all their hopes in our intercession with Your Majesty, which they believe will bring about their liberation, seeing that we can do nothing, despite all the firmness and constancy they have shown up to the present, will turn heretics through sheer despair; those who will persevere in the faith will be forced to flee for their lives and to come seeking the protection of Your Majesty and putting you to great expense by maintaining them in a manner proportionate to the royal munificence of Your Catholic Majesty, whom may our Lord keep for the good of the oppressed catholics of all christendom, which is the wish of these your most humble and loyal servants, from Louvain 3rd of December 1607.

TIRON   TIRCONELL

Meanwhile in Madrid letters from Brussels made King Philip realise that his orders requesting the Earls to remain in Flanders would have arrived too late to prevent their departure. Unaware until later that it had been possible for his ambassador, Guadaleste, to recall them, and wishing to avoid the embarrassment their presence in Spain would cause, King Philip's councillors advised that orders be sent to the Conde de Fuentes, governor of the Spanish territory of the Milanese, to the Conde de Oñate, Spanish ambassador at Turin, and to other Spanish officials, asking them to ensure that the Earls remained in Italy and away from the Spanish court while awaiting King Philip's decision concerning them.

In government and diplomatic circles, not only in Brussels and Madrid, but also in London and Rome, O Neill and his plans were the subject of much discussion, anxiety, fear and hope. On 15 November 1607, from his palace at Westminster, King James issued a proclamation, copies of which were circulated to his ambassadors for distribution abroad; this printed pamphlet was designed to turn public opinion against the Earls by describing them as conspirators and traitors, as men of low extraction who claimed titles of ancient nobility to which they were not entitled, and who were not to be believed in their complaints against their legitimate sovereign. In this document, King James declared solemnly, on the word of a king, 'verbo regio', that the Earls never had the slightest cause of complaint against him, not even in regard to religion; that in any case it was pointless to talk to them of religion for they were such barbarous people that they did not consider murder or illegitimate marriages to be criminal, and they measured courage and valour in terms of oppression and depredations; that their aim had been gradually to increase their strength at the expense of their neighbours so as to become capable of resisting all legitimate authority; that they had plotted rebellion and had employed various priests to solicit help from foreign princes; in conclusion, King James expressed his confidence that his proclamation would dispel the calumnies which those slanderous, treacherous and ungrateful men might spread against his just and moderate government.

In the face of persistent English pressure and in view of King Philip's disinclination to receive the Earls in Spain, it became necessary for the Archduke to show them a less open welcome; nevertheless they felt obliged to remain in Flanders until King Philip should reply to their letter and make known his decision. At the same time, on instructions from Rome, the Nuncio, Archbishop Bentivoglio, advised O Neill that he should rely completely on the King of Spain, and not on the Pope, for support for his plans; the Archbishop pointed out that the King had greater means at his disposal than were available to the Apostolic see and was, moreover, under obligation to O Neill for his past services.

The Pope was then Paul V who, as Cardinal Borghese, had been elected to the papacy in May 1605. Born in Rome in 1552, he studied law, held the offices of consistory advocate, papal abbreviator and legate to Bologna. On his return from a successful mission to Spain in June 1596, he was created Cardinal by Clement VIII. During his pontificate, a dispute with the Venetians led him to threaten the Doge with excommunication in April 1606, and the Papal States prepared to take arms against the Venetians. However, a reconciliation was effected through the mediation of the King of France. A Spanish ambassador in Rome described Pope Paul as 'parsimonious' and 'not very liberal'; however, he spent large sums of money on the embellishment of Rome and the Vatican and on the completion of the Church of St Peter. A man of imposing stature, he was described by a contemporary as 'so circumspect and reserved, that he is held for sombre.'

From London, the Spanish ambassador, Don Pedro de Zúñiga, encouraged King Philip to direct the Earls to Rome and reported on the reactions of King James and his ministers to the news that O Neill and O Donnell had been prevented from continuing their journey to Spain:

> *With regard to the Irish, it has sweetened their temper to know that Your Majesty does not wish that they go to Spain; if they were sent to Rome, it would restrain them* [King James and his ministers] *and make them live with care . . . The Pope . . . could be said to have sent for them. In Flanders, while this rumour is put about, His Highness might express the wish that they not remain there. In this way two advantages will be gained: the persecution will cease in Ireland and even here and, fearing trouble, they* [the English] *will certainly ask Your Majesty to act as mediator.*

This letter was discussed at a meeting of the Council of State in Madrid on 17 January 1608 as a result of which the following recommendations were submitted to the King:

> *The whole Council agrees that Your Majesty is obliged to protect those Earls because, when they were about to conclude a treaty with the Queen of England, which would have been to their advantage, they refrained from doing so because of the letters they received from Your Majesty. Since, as Don Pedro de Cuñiga points out, Rome is the most suitable place for them, it would be well that Your Majesty order them to go there. Your Majesty should write pressingly to the Pope in their favour and should remind him of the obligation he has to protect them. Your Majesty could order that, through the ambassador, they be given secretly the amount which they would have received had they come here, so that they may live with honour until the situation changes. If they go to Rome, having the freedom to do as they wish, the King of Great Britain could not find just cause for complaint against Your Majesty and their presence there will act as a restraint in the persecution of the catholics; on the contrary he will have reason to thank Your Majesty for not having allowed them in your territories, yet, in case of a break with England, the result will be the same as if they had come to Spain.*

Clearly the possibility of a renewal of war with England, and the value of O Neill's assistance in that eventuality was never far from the minds of the King's councillors; yet it was not their intention deliberately to provoke hostilities.

In accordance with the Council's recommendations which King Philip had accepted, letters were dispatched to Turin, Milan, Genoa and Barcelona with orders to the King's representatives to request the Earls, on arrival in any of those cities, to suspend their journey until further orders from the King. However, having decided that the Earls should go to Rome, it was not until the 14th of February that the Council met to discuss the amount of the allowance which would be granted to them and to decide who was to inform them of the King's wishes. The Council's advice to the King was as follows:

> *If the Earls are still in Flanders the Archduke should tell them Your Majesty wishes them to go to Rome and remain there. The Marques de Aytona should be instructed to represent to the Pope how fitting it would be that His Holiness protect and help these people who have lost their country and all they possessed for the catholic faith. If the Earls have already left Flanders, the Conde de Fuentes could tell them Your Majesty's wishes.*

> *As regards financial aid, it seems that the least one could give them would be 400 ducats a month to the Earl Oneill and 300 to the Earl Odoneill, and let this be paid to them punctually and in secret through the ambassador who should be supplied with the necessary funds for this purpose. The Conde de Fuentes could be sent instructions to give the Earls, should they be in need of money when they reach him, whatever he may think necessary to enable them to travel to Rome, for this is a pious cause; moreover, Your Majesty has a strong obligation to them considering that, when they were about to make peace with Queen Elizabeth, and greatly to their advantage, Your Majesty wrote to them to turn them from this purpose. Besides this, if we should break with the King of England, they could be of great service for they have great influence in Ireland.*

In Flanders, while awaiting the King's decision, the Earls' position had become increasingly difficult. They were spied upon by agents of the English ambassador; they knew that their presence was an embarrassment to the Archduke who was accused by King James of harbouring traitors to his crown, and they received less than positive reactions from the Nuncio who suggested that a visit to Rome would be inadvisable in view of the enmity which existed between the King of England and the Holy See. Finally, towards the middle of December 1607, they were told by Spínola that the Archduke wished them to leave his states, but it is clear, from a letter of the Spanish ambassador, that both Spínola and the ambassador considered the Archduke's decision to be 'very harsh'. For O Neill and O Donnell it was a serious set-back and they wrote to King Philip expressing their astonishment and indignation:

> *Having arrived in these States, in safe haven as we thought, for our sins and God permitting, another misfortune has befallen us. His Serene Highness orders that we leave his States so that he may keep a promise he made to the King of England and to his ministers . . . We believe that, in view of our past services, His Highness has the obligation of showing us more favour than this . . . As God is our witness, we would rather have chosen to die in our country than to see ourselves treated in this manner by a Prince in whom, after Your Majesty, we placed our greatest trust, and our concern is not so much for the danger to ourselves as for the sorrow and scandal this will cause to the other catholics, and the pleasure and satisfaction it will give the heretics to see us thus treated. The*

only consolation which remains to us is our hope that Your Majesty will not
abandon us, as we have cause to believe from the procedure of the Marques de
Guadaliste who has shown himself in this matter to be a very worthy minister of
such a Catholic Monarch as Your Majesty.

The Earls now had no option but to leave Flanders. They decided to
go to the Spanish territory of Milan, there to await King Philip's answer to
the letter they had sent to him, at his request, from Louvain. Arrangements
were made for the children who were to remain in Flanders with their
nurses, tutors and servants; among them were O Neill's two sons, John
and Brian, both under ten years of age, Hugh O Donnell, the infant heir of
the Earl of Tyrconnell, and the son of Cathbharr O Donnell, also named Hugh,
who was no more than three or four years of age.   On 28 February
1608, the Earls and their party, thirty-two of them on horseback and the
ladies in a coach, set out from Louvain.   No list of names of the travellers
on this journey has come to light, but the ladies' group very probably
consisted of O Neill's wife, the Countess Catherine Magennis, Nuala O
Donnell, sister of the Earl of Tyrconnell and wife of Niall Garbh O
Donnell, Róis O Dogherty, wife of Cathbharr O Donnell, and the beautiful
young daughter of O Neill, Bríd, who is mentioned later as being in Rome
with her parents and who may be the young lady 'of marriageable age'
noted by the Conde de Fuentes in his report of their arrival.

It is interesting to note that on the very day of their departure from
Louvain, O Neill and O Donnell took the time to address and sign an
appeal to the King of Spain on behalf of the Irish College of Douai.   The
following day saw them at Namur where they parted from Colonel Henry
O Neill who had accompanied them thus far. The slow pace of their
journey brought them to Nancy, capital of the duchy of Lorraine, on the
8th of March. Meanwhile, the watchful Edmonds reported O Neill's
departure to the Earl of Salisbury, and the Spanish ambassador in London
promptly wrote to King Philip describing the English government's
reaction to this news:

> *It was learned here that the Earl of Tiron's departure from Flanders was*
> *not to his pleasure and satisfaction; here it has caused great rejoicing. I know that*
> *they wish to kill him by poison or by any possible means, so I believe it is*
> *necessary to have him guarded. It will be well that Your Majesty keep him well*
> *disposed to your royal service for, to the English, he is a bridle. Their fear of him*
> *gnaws at their entrails and it will be all the greater if he may go to Rome, for they*
> *believe that if Your Majesty should send a hundred men with him to Ireland, all*
> *of that Kingdom would rise against them.*

Several weeks before O Neill's arrival at Nancy, the Duke of Lorraine
had received warning from Sir Thomas Edmonds that King James
expected that these 'fugitive rebels' of his would be refused entry to the
territory of Lorraine. But the Duke paid no heed and received O Neill and

his party with honour and a great display of hospitality. No doubt Ó Cianáin's words in praise of Lorraine were prompted by the Duke's generous behaviour:

> His country is thirty-five leagues in length, and it is a garden in the very centre of Christendom, giving neither obedience nor submission to any king or prince in the world, but ever steadfast, strong and unbending in the faith of God's Church.

When the Irish had passed on their way, the Duke answered Edmond's letter in terms which did not please the ambassador. He wrote to the Earl of Salisbury enclosing the Duke's letter, from which, Edmonds remarked, 'Your Lordship may perceive how much Tyrone's insinuations have wrought upon him.'

King James was so incensed by the favourable reception accorded to O Neill at Nancy that, when the Duke died shortly afterwards, on 14 May 1608, he sent no representative to the ceremonies of the funeral. This omission was commented upon by the French ambassador in London in a report to Paris:

> This King bears ill will towards the princes who have received and allowed freedom of travel in their country to the Earl of Thiron . . . A few days ago, speaking to one of the gentlemen of his household of the death of Monsieur de Lorraine, God grant him salvation, the King said that he would have more regret for the loss of that old man and would send messages of condolence to his children, had he not, before dying, caused him such grave displeasure by receiving the Earl and by the manner in which he did so. In fact, he is sending no one.

O Neill and his party continued their journey through Colmar, Basle and Lucerne which they reached on 16 March. On the following day they had the misfortune of losing a substantial sum of money, an incident which is described by Ó Cianáin:

> The next day, Saint Patrick's day precisely, the seventeenth of March, they went to another small town named Silenen. From that they advanced through the Alps. Now the mountains were laden and filled with snow and ice, and the roads and paths were narrow and rugged. They reached a high bridge in a very deep glen called the Devil's Bridge. One of O Neill's horses, which was carrying some of his money, about one hundred and twenty pounds, fell down the face of the high, frozen, snowy cliff which was in front of the bridge. Great labour was experienced in bringing up the horse alone, but the money decided to remain blocking the violent, deep, destructive torrent which flows under the bridge through the middle of the glen.

The following day, when further efforts to retrieve the money proved unsuccessful, the attempt was abandoned and the travellers continued on their way through Andermatt, the St Gothard Pass, Bellinzona and Lugano. On March 22nd they reached Como and the next day, after a journey of over three weeks they arrived at the city of Milan. Ó Cianáin records their arrival:

> On Sunday the twenty-third of March, after having heard Mass, they proceeded to the great remarkable famous city of Milan, a distance of eight leagues over good roads, the day being wet and very stormy. After their journey they remained resting until the following Wednesday. A great respected earl, one of the most excellent soldiers in the world in his time also, as his victory and fortune in battle and good luck showed clearly and evidently to Christendom, Count de Fuentes by name, was chief-governor and representative of the king of Spain over that city and over all Lombardy. He sent the king's ambassador at Lucerne, who happened to be in the city, to welcome them and to receive them with honour. On Wednesday the nobles went in person into the presence of the earl. He received them with honour and respect. There were many noblemen and a very great guard on either side of him. They remained three full weeks in the city. During that time the earls had great honour shown them.

A report of the Conde de Fuentes on the arrival of the Earls adds a few more interesting details; it is addressed to King Philip on 13 April 1608, the day after the Earls' departure from Milan on their way to Rome:

> The Earls of Tiron and Tirconel arrived here before holy week and, in accordance with Your Majesty's orders, I feasted them and treated them with care in as discreet and secret a manner as possible, in order both to assure them of the generosity and compassion of Your Majesty and to make them amenable to Your Majesty's wishes . . . I felt the greatest pity for them; one of them brings a sister of marriageable age, and another a wife and son; they bring also many persons who would not be parted from them. They arrived in great distress from the hardship of the journey and in such need that it was necessary to pay their hostelries and to give them money for the journey.

From the correspondence of the Nuncio at Brussels, it is clear that, on leaving Flanders, O Neill had been determined to remain in Milan until he received definite orders from King Philip to proceed either to Spain or to Rome; this is borne out in a letter written by the Earls from Milan on 2 April to the Archbishop of Armagh, Peter Lombard, who was then in Rome:

> As regards our going to Rome (as we wrote in our last letter to you) we do not intend to undertake that journey without first receiving orders to that effect from the Catholic King so that he might not have an excuse to abandon us and to leave us to the sole patronage of the Pope . . . Therefore we do not wish to decide anything with regard to that journey until we have received an answer and a directive from the King.

Consequently it was not without question that the Earls eventually agreed to proceed to Rome, and they made clear to the Conde de Fuentes, when he informed them of the King's wishes, how reluctant they were:

> *Although at the beginning they were somewhat reluctant to go to Rome without seeing a letter from Your Majesty ordering them to do so, I managed to convince them and they left yesterday. I told them that it would be of greater advantage to them to await in Rome Your Majesty's decision concerning them, and this could be hastened if they begged the Pope to write to Your Majesty. At the same time I assured them that they would be well received and helped there, and that Your Majesty's great kindness would not fail them.*

The Earls were forced to rely on the assurances of the Conde de Fuentes but, so that King Philip should be under no misapprehension, they wrote to him explaining their position:

> *Now that we are leaving the dominions of Your Majesty (in order to comply with your royal wishes) we beg you to send to Rome without delay an answer concerning our affairs. Although it is very much against our wishes that we are going there, when we remember how we have served Your Majesty and what we have lost by taking up arms in your royal service and in that of the Catholic Church, we are convinced that Your Majesty is not causing us to leave your dominions in order to abandon us, but on the contrary so as to be in a position to help us with greater facility and secrecy, as the Conde de Fuentes has indicated to us.*

This letter was accompanied by two memorials from the Earls (see Appendix, pp. 134-138), one of which repeats much of the contents of their letter from Louvain, while adding a few more details of the events which led to their escape, and reiterating their request for military aid with which to return to Ireland. The second memorial describes the history of their race and recalls the Milesian legend, which was then accepted as historical fact both in Spain and in Ireland and according to which the Irish and the Spaniards are of the same race and have the same origins. There are many references to this belief in Spanish records relating to Ireland, and Ó Cianáin recalls it in passing when, lamenting the deaths of Ruairí and Cathbharr O Donnell and of Maguire and MacMahon, he refers to them as the descendants of *Míl Espáinne*.

Before leaving Flanders, the Earls had decided to send Matthew Tully to Madrid as their representative at the Spanish court. He may have left Louvain ahead of them, because on 13 February, a fortnight before the Earls' departure, he received permission from the Archduke to travel to Spain; and he was probably accompanied by the Franciscan Dr Robert Chamberlain who also received permission to go to Spain on the same date. At any rate, Matthew Tully was in Madrid by 26 April, when he presented to the King his letters of recommendation from the Earls of

Tyrone and Tyrconnell, together with a memorial on their behalf requesting an answer to their letter sent to the King from Louvain and asking that, in the meantime, provision be made for their maintenance and that of their families and followers.

It was not long before the English ambassador in Spain, Sir Charles Cornwallis, was aware of the presence of the Earls' envoy in Madrid. On 29 April he wrote to the Privy Council in London concerning the Earls' reception in Milan and the arrival of Matthew Tully in Madrid. In this letter, the ambassador refers to Matthew as *Mack Ogg,* and elsewhere as *Mag Ogy,*   a corruption of his name in Irish, Matha óg:

> *Having lately gathered amongst the Irish here that the fugitive Earls have been in Milan, and there much feasted by the Conde de Fuentes, I expostulated it with the secretary of state, who answered that they had not yet had any understanding of their being there . . . I sent sithence by Cottington, my secretary, concerning one Mack Ogg, lately come hither, as I have been advised, to solicit for these people; which was, that as I hoped they would have no participation with the principals, whose crimes had now been made so notorious in their own countries . . . I likewise assured myself that, in their own wisdoms, they would not hold it fit His Majesty here should give harbour or ear to any of their ministers, and especially to that of Mack Ogg, who could not be supposed but to have had a hand in their traitorous purposes; having been the man and the means, in person, to withdraw them by sea out of their own countries, in such undutiful and suspicious manner . . . To this his answer was, that this Mack Ogg, as far as he yet could comprehend, neither brought letter in his pocket nor word in his mouth from any of them;   that he hath been an ancient* entretenido *to the King, and hath in these wars of the Low Countries spent much blood in his service; that his errand is to recover his entertainment, which there of late they have taken from him. By God's grace, I will keep a vigilant eye upon the ways which that man will tread in.*

Of course, the Spanish Secretary of State knew well that Matthew Tully had brought messages from O Neill and O Donnell; only three days earlier the Council of State had discussed a memorial presented by Tully on behalf of the Earls.   In December of that year, the ambassador was still reporting that he could receive 'no answer to his complaint of their harbouring and enlarging their lands to Mack Ogg, so notoriously known to be a solicitor for Tyrone and a writer against the King's estate.'

CHAPTER FOUR

The Earls in Rome

On 29 April 1608, O Neill, O Donnell and their companions made their entry into Rome. Shortly before their arrival the Spanish ambassador in Rome, Marqués de Aytona, had an interview with the Pope, following which he reported to King Philip:

> I have represented to His Holiness, on behalf and in the name of Your Majesty, how fitting and proper it would be that His Holiness protect and help those who, for the catholic faith and in defence of our holy religion, have lost their possessions and country and everything they owned. I also told His Holiness that the Earls' presence here may act as a deterrent against the persecution of the Catholics in England. His Holiness replied that he would honour and favour them as much as he could. I think that he will give them nothing, or very little, because the apostolic treasury is very low, and His Holiness is not very liberal . . . Your Majesty orders me to spread the rumour that His Holiness has sent for the Earls and will give them great help and protection as people who, for the service of God and his holy faith, lost everything they had. The Pope does not wish me to say that he has sent for them but that they come of their own accord to seek refuge with him.

The Earls' arrival in Rome is described by Ó Cianáin who records that they were met at the Ponte Molle on the outskirts of the city by Archbishop Peter Lombard and by representatives of Cardinals who brought with them fifteen coaches, all except a few of which were drawn by six horses. They entered the city by the Porta del Populo, drove through the principal streets of Rome and went directly to the basilica of St Peter, where they worshipped at the seven privileged altars. Afterwards they proceeded to a palace which the Pope had set apart for them; this was probably the Palazzo dei Penitenzieri which is situated between the Via della Conciliazione and the Borgo Santo Spirito. The final stage of the Earls' journey was observed by a spy employed by Sir Henry Wotton, the English ambassador at Venice, who had earlier reported to Salisbury that he had sent to Milan an agent 'who shall accompany Tirone and his gang over all Italy.' Consequently on 9 May, Wotton was able to send the following information to Salisbury concerning O Neill's arrival in Rome:

Tyrone arrived on the 29th of April. About two miles out of the town he was met by eight coaches, and six horses to every coach, sent by the Cardinals Montalto, Farnese, Colonna and Barberini. The English papists by commandment of the Pope went to meet him, and he was thus conducted to St. Peter's church in the Vatican where he first set foot on ground, and so, after a short Ave Maria, was brought to a palace close by furnished for him by the Pope, who defrays all his charges.

The Earls were received with every mark of respect, kindness and honour by the Pope and by the Cardinals. However, the Pope did not defray all their charges; according to a later report they received from him no more than one hundred crowns a month. As for King Philip, the inadequacy of the amount offered to the Earls on his behalf was yet another set-back for them, not, as they pointed out, that they wished to make a display of pomp and undue wealth, but because 'we know it is injurious to Your Majesty and harmful to our cause that the English should witness the lack of necessities from which we suffer here.' The Spanish ambassador's report of 22 May 1608 informed King Philip of the Earls' disappointment and indignation at the amount offered to them:

Many days ago I wrote to Your Majesty that the Earls of Tiron and Tirconel arrived in this city and that the Pope gave them a house but nothing else . . . I wished to give them what Your Majesty ordered, 400 ducats to the Earl of Tiron and 300 to the Earl of Tirconel for the first month, but they showed such contempt for this amount that their majordomos, by order of their masters, refused to accept it. The Earls felt as injured as if the grant were not very good and were so aggrieved that they wished to go to Madrid. I held them back with kind words but I do not think that will suffice if they are without money. They are very unreasonable and say that the Duke of Ahumala [i.e. Aumale] receives 2,000 ducats each month from Your Majesty and that both of them deserve the same, which would be 4,000 ducats between the two. They say they have served more than the Duke of Ahumala. Yesterday one of those who came with them told me that they would not take less than 1,000 a month each. I was really vexed. I did my best to placate them and they consented to accept the money, but consider it only as a token of what Your Majesty will give them when well informed of their needs . . .

Their misfortunes have done so little to humble them that they take as an insult not to be given immediately all they demand . . . I think it might be well in many respects if they could be sent somewhere else away from this city. They have strong feelings on what is due to their blood and position and here in Rome the eyes of the world are on them; also, in this city everything is very expensive . . . I send to Your Majesty the letter the Earls wrote to me.

The Duke of Aumale was one of the many prominent people whom O Neill and O Donnell met in Flanders and it would not have been difficult for them to find out the amount of his pension. It was certainly very substantial, for a letter of 29 April 1608 from the Archduke to King Philip mentions the fact that Aumale had just been paid 4,000 ducats, and refers to some arrears of pension owed to him which amounted to 50,000 ducats.

As regards their own maintenance, O Neill and O Donnell had discussed with the Conde de Fuentes in Milan the amount of money they would need for living expenses in Rome while awaiting the King's decision with regard to an Irish expedition, and they had expressed the view that 2,500 ducats a month between them would not be sufficient. Nevertheless Fuentes suggested to King Philip that they be given 'a little more than half that amount.' The Spanish Council recommended even less. The sum of 700 ducats which was offered to the Earls on behalf of the King by the ambassador in Rome fell far short of their needs and they asked that separate allowances be made for certain members of their group, but this was denied. We know that their group numbered over fifty, consequently the allowance granted by the King would have averaged about 14 ducats a month for each person. Bearing in mind that the pay of a private soldier varied from 6 to 8 crowns a month and that the highest pay of a captain was then 40 crowns, the dismay expressed by the Earls is not difficult to understand. The difference in value between the ducat and the crown, or *escudo,* was very little. In coinage of *vellón,* an alloy of silver and copper, which was the usual currency, the ducat was worth 11 *reales* and the crown was the equivalent of 10 *reales.* When gold coinage was used, the fact was noted, for the gold crown had a higher value of 16 *reales;* there is no indication that this might have been the case with regard to the Earls' allowance. Therefore, assuming that there were no more than fifty persons with the Earls, the average maintenance payment for each of them was equivalent only to double the pay of a private soldier.

More important to O Neill and O Donnell than considerations of mere physical comfort would have been the appearance which they presented to the world at large in a city such as Rome. It was necessary for the success of their cause that their appearance should inspire confidence and be in keeping with their standing, as much for the encouragement of their supporters as for the demoralisation of their enemies. This was all the more important in view of the proclamation of King James, numerous copies of which had been circulated by English ambassadors in Europe and in which the Earls were described as persons of low birth and as traitors and deceivers who claimed titles of ancient nobility to which they were not entitled. Indeed, it was probably with this proclamation in mind that O Neill and O Donnell drew up the document which they headed: 'Description of the lands of the Earls of Tyron and Tyrconel and brief account of their race and their descendence.' This document was sent by them to the King of Spain from Milan.

In Rome, with no other source of income but the allowance from King Philip and the small additional grant from the Pope, the Irish exiles found themselves in debt within a few months of their arrival. By then, however, the Spanish ambassador, Aytona, had come to realise the inadequacy of their grant and it is interesting to note the change of attitude reflected in his letters to the King. In May 1608, the ambassador had complained that the Earls were unreasonable and had made no secret of his annoyance with them; six months later he wrote to the King:

> *I beg Your Majesty to give them some extra financial aid. Their grant is barely sufficient for their food and in other respects they suffer great want. They are so poor that one must have compassion for them. The Pope gives them a house but not one stick of furniture and they have neither beds nor chairs. The unfortunates have not money to buy such bare necessities and, as there are many Irish with the Earl, a large sum would be necessary to buy even what would be needed so that they might not be forced to sleep on the floors.*

It was not, however, until two and a half years later, in May 1611, that O Neill's grant was increased by one hundred ducats a month.

In the early summer of 1608, King Philip received from his ambassador in London, Don Pedro de Zúñiga, the news of Cahir O Dogherty's rising in Ireland. Its effects in England, as seen by the ambassador, are described in a letter of 26 May:

> *With this rising in Ireland the English are in such a state of fear that I understand they will give the Irish freedom of conscience. While the Earl of Tyrone is alive in Rome they will always fear, for they assure me that if he returns to Ireland with ten men, the whole kingdom would take up arms.*

Shortly afterwards Don Pedro expressed the view, so often put forward by O Neill in his memorials to King Philip, that the weakened state of the English government offered an excellent opportunity for the re-establishment of the catholic religion in Ireland as well as in England:

> *What is happening in Ireland has shown very clearly the state of affairs here, for they have sent only 800 or 1,000 men over there, and no money. Here, there is not one penny. The Earl of Salsberi is tearing at his beard and heartily regrets having accepted the post of treasurer. He has told his closest friends that it will kill him and bring dishonour upon his name . . . What I can certainly assure Your Majesty is that, according to my soundings, the state of this country is such that we may promise ourselves the happiest outcome if His Holiness would send Tyron to Ireland. Here, they are without money. The Scots are hated and there is a terrible disunion between English and Scots because the latter favour the Prince [of Wales] and the English favour the Duke of Jorque [York] and, on top of all that, Ireland is in a state of half revolt and will be completely so, if it should come to be known that help would come with Tiron.*

Don Pedro added that, while speaking of these matters with *El Cid*, which, as we have seen, was the ambassador's code name for the Earl of Northampton, the latter exclaimed on two occasions that, if the Pope and the King of Spain did not avail of this opportunity, such another would not come in their lifetime.

News of the initial successes of O Dogherty's rising in Ireland had reached the Earls in Italy; the Spanish ambassador in London had even written directly to his colleague in Rome on the matter. O Neill and O Donnell were anxiously awaiting further news of events in Ireland and an answer from King Philip. It was now seven months since they had sent the first of several memorials to the King. At first they had waited patiently for a reply which they still hoped would be favourable, and they had indeed need of patience for, at that time, almost two months would elapse between the dispatch of a letter from Rome to Madrid and the receipt of its reply. Now, however, the Earls must have realised that the opportunity offered by O Dogherty's rising would be lost unless immediate help were available. On 9 July 1608 they wrote to King Philip in urgent and accusing terms:

Señor, by order of Your Majesty we wrote from Flanders saying what our requests were, how anxious the Irish Catholics were to show their zeal in defence of the holy catholic faith and how they hoped that Your Majesty would deliver them from the intolerable persecution and tyranny they are suffering. From Milan we informed Your Majesty of our arrival there and that the Conde de Fuentes had told us it was Your Majesty's wish that we come to Rome. We also begged to be told, as soon as possible, Your Majesty's decision with regard to our affairs. We have not yet received any reply.

Although up to the present we have waited patiently, believing that Your Majesty's delay was due to the great care and consideration being given to the matter, we can no longer disguise our feelings.

We have been informed that in Ulster four thousand of our people have revolted and are causing great losses to the English. The rising is spreading to the other provinces for, knowing that we are here, all firmly believe that Your Majesty will not fail to send help with us to Ireland.

In the letter we wrote from Flanders we gave Your Majesty all details on this matter and, for greater safety, we also gave to the Marques de Aytona a memorial for Your Majesty containing all information on the affairs of Ireland from the beginning until the present and begging Your Majesty not to allow that such a good opportunity be lost.

The only wish of the catholics of Ireland is to be free of their troubles and to become subjects of Your Majesty. We declare that you will lose much more by allowing the destruction of a kingdom of catholics who wish to serve you than by dissembling and compromising with the English, thereby causing the loss of that kingdom. And if Ireland is lost (as it must be if help is not sent) Your Majesty will then have proof that the English do not keep their word. They will commit

*again the same excesses and atrocities for they are only awaiting the opportunity;
and then the Irish, Your Majesty's servants, will not be there. But if you were to
send them some help now, and indeed the Irish wish to open all the ports to
Spanish help, within a few days Ireland would belong to Your Majesty and the
English and the Dutch would be held in check.*

*If Your Majesty is not moved by reasons of state and your own interest, we
humbly beg that you be moved by christian feelings to defend the Irish nation so
that its people may not lose the catholic faith which they have professed and
upheld for centuries. If now, through lack of help from a christian Prince, the
Irish should lose this faith, they may well call God and his saints to witness that
it was not because their courage failed them. Many times the Irish have taken up
arms in defence of their faith. Perhaps others may be called upon to answer to
God for having failed to help them . . .*

May God keep Your Majesty for the benefit of all christians.
Rome, 9th of July 1608.

                TIRON   *TIRCONELL.*

The Earls believed that the main obstacle to their plan of a landing in
Ireland was Spain's reluctance to act openly against England and they
recognised the Pope's unwillingness to help in financing the expedition.
They now sought an audience with the Pope and asked his permission to
suggest to King Philip that any help Spain might consider sending to
Ireland could be sent in the Pope's name. On 22 July 1608 this suggestion
was duly forwarded to Philip through the Spanish ambassador with yet
another memorial from O Neill and O Donnell.   It is ironical that, while
these efforts were being made in Rome to induce King Philip to provide
the help so urgently needed, Philip himself was considering what arguments might be used to convince the Pope that it was his responsibility to
send help to Ireland. On 29 July 1608 he wrote to his ambassador in Rome:

*Concerning affairs in Ireland and the troubled state of England, it is clear
that any effort made now to re-establish the holy faith in those parts would have
a favourable chance of success and would be most pleasing in the eyes of God.
The best way to achieve this purpose would be through the co-operation of the
Irish Earls in Rome. Ireland belongs to the Apostolic See from ancient times and
this should be sufficient reason to move a generous pontiff who would wish to
leave a good name to posterity. I have wished to advise you of this and I also
command you to execute the following orders with the greatest discretion and
secrecy:*

*Father Personio, whose prudence and talents are known to you, is at
present in Rome. Procure, as coming from you, that he raise this matter with the
Pope and that he incline the Irish Earls to do the same. He should incite the Pope
to recover this patrimony of the Church by reminding him that in the time of
Pope Gregory XIII another similar enterprise was highly successful and that
His Holiness would not be fulfilling his obligations or accomplishing the duties
of his God-given office if he did not attend to a matter which is of such
consequence to the Church or if he allowed this opportunity to pass.*

Father *Personio,* whom the King mentions in this letter, was the English Jesuit Robert Parsons who had been very active in Rome on behalf of English catholics. However, the Pope was not inclined to fall in with these plans; the negotiations came to nothing and O Neill warned King Philip against allowing plans for an expedition to Ireland to become known to any Englishman for, he explained:

> *The said Father* [Parsons] *is a very good and virtuous religious, neverthe-less he is in correspondence with many English people whom he believes are honest, and they are not all as good as he is. Among so many English people there is always a spy and one who will play with both hands. Although it is true that for our purpose it is necessary that we should find out from them the state of affairs in England, we cannot let them know what we plan to do in Ireland, for under no circumstances do they wish to see the advancement of our country, and we know this with certitude through long experience.*

Although pressure from England had been successful in keeping the Earls away from Spain and from personal contact with King Philip, King James and his ministers still feared that O Neill might contrive to lead an expedition to Ireland. In view of this, they looked upon the Irish regiment in Flanders with suspicion. Sir Thomas Edmonds in Brussels referred to it as 'the gunpowder regiment' and already in 1608, at the request of Salisbury, Chichester had 'considered the means that must be used to break the Irish regiment in Flanders.' However, it was not in Spain's interest to allow the destruction of a regiment of seasoned soldiers whose importance, in case of a break with England, had already been noted by the Spanish Council of State. Consequently when O Neill from Rome and Colonel Henry from Brussels, reported the activities of English spies in the regiment, steps were taken to remove the suspects, on other pretexts as Henry had asked, so that the English would not know their spies had been discovered. Later efforts to destroy the regiment were equally unsuccessful and in 1612 the English ambassador in Brussels wrote to London: 'The Irish regiment is certainly maintained for no other purpose than to invade England in case of trouble between the King of England and the King of Spain.'

The summer of 1608 brought illness and death to many of O Neill's companions in exile. Ó Cianáin, whose chronicle of events ends in November of that year, recounts that in the month of July a small group of them decided to leave Rome for a few days to take a change of air, no doubt to escape from the oppressive heat of the city. Among them were Ruairí O Donnell, Earl of Tyrconnell, his brother Cathbharr, and O Neill's son Hugh, Baron of Dungannon:

> *The three set out, taking with them a page and a footman. Alas! their trip was attended with ill luck and misfortune. They went to a certain town on the sea coast named Ostia, on the bank of the Tiber, fifteen miles from Rome. They*

stayed for two days and nights on both sides of the river. The Reverend Doctor Domhnall Ó Cearbhaill followed them. These noblemen next returned to Rome. Their journey to Ostia was no source of rejoicing to their friends, for all are agreed that that particular place is one of the worst and most unhealthy for climate in all Italy. Indeed, it was not long until it proved so to them, for the Earl took a hot, fiery, violent fever on the eighteenth of July in 1608, the day of the week being Friday. On Saturday, the following day, Cathbharr, the son of Ó Domhnaill, caught the same fever. On the Monday afterwards, the Baron was stricken with it, and Domhnall Ó Cearbhaill in a short time after him. The page and the footman who were with them both got the fever in a very short time. The Earl had a violent sickness and great pain during a period of eleven days. He made a full confession and received the Holy Sacrament. His soul separated from his body and he died, by the grace of God and the Church, after victory over the world and the devil, about midnight on Monday. On the following day, Tuesday the twenty-ninth of July, the feast of Saint Martha, the Earl was buried in the monastery of San Pietro Montorio. A large and splendid funeral in grand procession was ordered by his Holiness the Pope, and on either side of the body there were large numbers of lighted waxen torches and sweet, sad, sorrowful singing. It was enwrapped in the habit of Saint Francis, as he himself had ordered that it should be put about him. Muiris, the Earl's page, died on the third of August. On the eighteenth of the same month Domhnall Ó Cearbhaill, Doctor of Divinity, the son of Uaithne Ó Cearbhaill of Magh Dreithne in Urmhumha, died.

Also in August of that year occurred the deaths of Maguire, who had been instrumental in bringing to Ireland the boat in which the Earls made their escape, and of Seamus MacMahon, one of those who had sailed with them from Lough Swilly. On 7 June 1608 they left Rome to go to Naples and eventually to Spain. Ó Cianáin does not tell us the reason for their journey to the Italian port, which was then a Spanish possession, but in view of the fact that a number of Irish exiles resided at Naples where they had been assigned grants or pensions by the King of Spain, it is possible that Maguire and MacMahon wished to consult some knowledgeable friends of theirs with regard to their intended journey to Spain. Among the Irish based at Naples was the one-time Recorder of Cork, William Meade, or Guillermo Miagh as he was known in Spain, who would have been in a position to advise the travellers, for he himself had visited the Spanish court in 1603 to request help from King Philip on behalf of the catholics of Ireland;   he was held in such high esteem by his compatriots that they entrusted him with several missions and, later, he acted as O Neill's envoy in Spain. Another Irishman who received his salary from the treasury of Naples and who could have been of use to the travellers, was Captain Juan Phalveo, or Falvey.   Captain Falvey was in a happier financial position than most of his compatriots abroad; his will, made in Madrid some years later, reveals that he had an account with the bank of Pavía in Lombardy where he had a deposit of 7,000 gold crowns.   At any rate, having spent some time in Naples, Maguire and MacMahon left for Genoa where they intended to embark for Spain, but they became ill and died in that city within six hours of each other on 12 August 1608; and yet further grief was in store for the exiles for, as Ó Cianáin records:

> *The Baron* [Hugh, son of O Neill] *and the son of Ó Domhnaill* [Cathbharr, younger brother of Tyrconnell] *lay in the fever during all that time. By order of the doctors, they were brought to a splendid palace on Monte Citorio that they might have air different and better than that of the Borgo, where they had been up to that time. When they had been some time there, the son of O Domhnaill died on the fifteenth day of September. It may well be believed that it was not through good fortune or the best of fate that it happened to Ireland that so many of the choicest of the descendants of Míl Easpáinne died suddenly, one after another, in a foreign and strange land, far removed from their own native soil. The son of O Domhnaill was buried in the habit of St. Francis, after having had a great funeral and splendid cortege following him in procession, in the same monastery of San Pietro Montorio, in the same manner as the Earl, and close to his tomb.*

O Neill's son, the Baron of Dungannon, recovered from his illness, only to die the following year. So much misfortune within so short a time must have seemed an ill-omen to the Irish exiles who anxiously awaited the opportunity of a return to their lands. From Madrid, the English ambassador wrote to London concerning the death of the Earl of Tyrconnell:

> *The death of Tyrconnell in Rome is now confirmed by the mourning vestures of the agents and followers of him and his traitorous company that are here. Mag Ogy . . ., their agent, sometimes nourished with a small ration in the Conde de Villamediana's house, and no otherwise reckoned of in those times than his birth and his quality deserved, walks now these streets (in black weeds) in fashion of a grandee, followed by two pages, and accompanied by four others of his countrymen in the like attire. A sign that they are here no unwelcome guests.*

CHAPTER FIVE

Plantation in Ulster

By September 1608 it had become clear that neither Pope Paul nor King Philip showed any willingness to support an Irish expedition, and the uneasy peace between Spain and England was still holding. Nevertheless, O Neill's presence on the continent, his unceasing efforts to organise the reconquest of his country, and O Dogherty's rebellion, had a disturbing effect in England. There were signs that King James would prefer to have O Neill return to Ireland on terms of reconciliation rather than have him at large and perhaps eventually successful in his aims. Late in August 1608 the Spanish Council of State advised King Philip as follows:

> Don Pedro de Çuñiga has confirmed that the English are so disturbed about the rising that they offer to pardon the Earls and tolerate the catholic religion in their estates. He says also that they are considering sending a person to Rome, so it will be well to advise the Marques de Aytona of this. In such an event he should procure that the Pope obtain liberty of conscience from the English at least for the two provinces of Ulster and Connaught.
>
> So that the Earls be not discouraged, the Marques must not let them think that help will not be sent to them. If they ask for an answer to their letter, let them be told to apply to the Marques. For very good reasons they should not be answered in writing. The Marques should be told to console and encourage them.

On 13 September 1608 O Neill sent another memorial to King Philip repeating his plea for help but adding that if this request were denied, he asked the King to obtain for him a reconciliation with the King of England.

It was now a year since O Neill had left Ireland. During that time he had sent many memorials to Philip and his ministers describing the state of affairs in Ireland and asking for the help which Spain had promised and which Philip had never positively refused. The only replies he was given were transmitted orally by the Spanish ambassador and suggested indecision and procrastination on the part of the King: *the matter is under consideration; the time is not opportune; Spain cannot yet act openly in the matter; funds are insufficient; Pope Paul is being asked for the help needed.* Always, however, O Neill was given to understand that Spain only awaited a better opportunity to give him the support for which he asked. Consequently he was expected to remain in Rome until such an opportunity arose.

By the end of 1608 O Neill's patience had worn thin. He was now a virtual prisoner in Rome. The delays in correspondence with Ireland, Flanders and Madrid must have been exasperating, but to leave Rome for Flanders without King Philip's approval was out of the question. The basis of O Neill's policy was to manoeuvre the King into a commitment either covertly to back his return to Ireland with a military force, or to authorise negotiations for a reconciliation with King James. In either case, and regardless of the consequences, King Philip would have an obligation to O Neill and to the cause of the Irish catholics. It is evident that O Neill considered the support of Spain essential, in the short term, to the over-throw of English rule in Ireland and, in the long term, as a guarantee against further attempts by England to colonise Ireland.

Since the immediate possibility of returning to Ireland with an army seemed out of the question, O Neill now appeared to be considering what advantages could be gained by a reconciliation with the King of England. It may well be that he had no intention of going through with the proposed reconciliation, but thought that his apparent compliance with Philip's wishes would gain him permission to go to Flanders. However, on 4 January 1609 he wrote to King Philip:

Señor, although since I left my country I have written often and regularly to Your Majesty, in all this time I have received no answer. Nevertheless I cannot cease to do so until Your Majesty be pleased to do me the favour of answering me in some definite way. And so I beg you as I did in my last letter to let me leave this country in which I do not wish to remain any longer, even were I in comfortable circumstances, much less in the misery which I suffer and of which I informed Your Majesty many times without ever having received satisfaction.

I know well that when we first left our country we could have obtained a reconciliation, however short its duration, with the King of England who was then well disposed to give it. We did not ask for it, always hoping that we and the afflicted catholics of Ireland would fare better by relying on your help, and Your Majesty knows how willingly and faithfully we have always served you and how much we have lost in that service.

I humbly beg, if Your Majesty cannot help us in any other way, that at least you obtain for me and for the young Earl of Tyrconell a reconciliation with the King of England and, while this is being negotiated, let Your Majesty be pleased to order that I leave this country where I know that I cannot live much longer. I can be of more service in my own country or anywhere else rather than here in Rome where I can only bury my bones with those of the other Irish who have died here. May God keep Your Majesty for the benefit of Christendom.

TIRON.

It was not until four months later that O Neill was given an answer to this letter. Philip wrote to his ambassador:

> *You will tell the Earl of Tiron that his letters have been received and that for whatever negotiations he wishes it is better that he should be in Rome than elsewhere. He should state the terms of reconciliation that would suit him for I shall be pleased to know them so that I may take a decision on the matter.*

In the meantime the well-informed English ambassador in Madrid, Sir Charles Cornwallis, reported to London: 'Tyrone is endeavouring to get the King [*of Spain*] to mediate for the restoration to him of his country, with the King's pardon and favour.' However, he added that he thought King Philip would not 'interfere in a matter which he knows to be of so evil a savour in England.'

In January 1609, King James issued orders for the plantation and distribution of the lands of O Neill and O Donnell and their followers among English and Scots settlers. The King's orders were printed under the title: 'A Collection of such Orders and Conditions as are to be observed by the Undertakers upon the Distribution and Plantation of the escheated lands of Ulster.' When this news reached Rome, Father Florence Conry, who had recently been appointed Archbishop of Tuam, wrote with indignation to the secretary of the Spanish Council of State, Andrés de Prada:

> *Since dispatching my last letter to you, a small English pamphlet has come to my hands. It was printed in London a few months ago and contains the articles by which the King of England declares, without stating the reasons, to have confiscated and appropriated the lands of the Earls of Tiron and Tirconnel to the extent of six counties. The English King offers these lands in perpetuity for themselves and their descendants to any Scots and English who may wish to take possession of them provided that they comply with the following conditions:*
>
> *They must first swear that the King is head of the Church; they may not sublease these lands to any Irish of the ancient race of Ireland; each county must have schools for the instruction of youth in the Calvinistic religion; instead of priests all parish churches must have heretical ministers who will consume the income of the heretical church.*
>
> *This is the substance of the contents of the pamphlet and I have wished to inform you of it that you may see how much reason the Earl of Tiron had to urge His Catholic Majesty all this past year to return him to his estates by some means or, at least, to take some decision on the matter before this confiscation was made. The Earl believes that this would not have happened if the English had not seen that the King of Spain is not so inclined to help him now as was at first expected. The Earl blames me somewhat for not having allowed him to press His Majesty more than he did for I always held him back, as I felt that the Earl was making himself clear enough and that His Majesty was considering the matter to good purpose, as I trust that now he will. With the help of God and the assistance of His Catholic Majesty, who will not consent to such an extraordi-*

nary and renewed extirpation and oppression of catholics and of the holy faith, I hope that those iniquitous articles of the King of England will resolve themselves into air.

The pamphlet which I send translated into Spanish and the letter which the Earl is writing to His Majesty will show you what good cause he and the catholics have for complaint and sorrow and how little is to be expected from those heretics. May God keep you as I wish.
Rome, May 1st, 1609.

Fray Florencio Conryo
Archbishop of Tuam.

As soon as O Neill received the news that Philip wished to know his terms of reconciliation with King James, he lost no time in forwarding these to Madrid and, within a few days, Archbishop Conry left Rome for the Spanish capital taking with him, together with a long memorial from O Neill, the following letter for King Philip:

Señor, after all this time Your Majesty has done me the favour of ordering that I send my terms of reconciliation. If I were in Madrid I could inform Your Majesty of this matter in detail and answer any difficulties that may arise, but, as I am so far away, I think it would be necessary that I send a person who would speak on my behalf and explain everything, although, since I left my country, I have done so myself many times by letter. For this purpose I have asked the Archbishop of Tuam, the bearer of this letter, to go to Madrid. He is well acquainted with all the circumstances and has, for a long time past, been engaged in the affairs of Ireland which concern Your Majesty's service. I humbly beg you to be pleased to order that the said Archbishop be given access to the court during the negotiations of this matter which is of such importance to the service of God and of Your Majesty. May God keep Your Majesty for the good of Christendom. Rome, 9th of June, 1609.

TIRON.

At the same time O Neill sent word to his son in Flanders, Colonel Henry, to join the Archbishop in Madrid. The time was opportune, for the difficult peace negotiations between Spanish Flanders and the United Provinces had finally culminated in a twelve years' truce signed at Antwerp in April of that year. On 13 August 1609, Henry received permission from the Archduke Albert to absent himself from his post for six months, and on the same date, no doubt at O Neill's request, the Archduke wrote to the Duke of Lerma in support of the Earl's cause and in recommendation of Colonel Henry:

Muy Illustre Señor, I am writing to the King, my Lord, begging His Majesty to act as mediator with the King of Great Britain that the lands of the Earl of Tiron in Ireland be not confiscated for it is understood that the said King has given orders for their confiscation. Since there are so many reasons to give help, protection and assistance to the said Earl in his concerns, I ask your lordship to obtain this from His Majesty who promised me that he would do so with all willingness.

For the same purpose Colonel Don Henrique O Neill is going to Spain. He is the son of the Earl of Tiron; he serves here with a regiment of Irish infantry and has done so for close on four years with so much valour and in such a manner that, both on this account and because of his very promising behaviour, he deserves all favour. Therefore I also ask your lordship to be of assistance to him in obtaining His Majesty's favour, assuring you that I shall duly esteem your intervention in both these matters. May God keep your lordship as I wish, from Brussels on the 13th of August 1609.

At your lordship's orders,

Alberto.

The Archduke's letter is written with careful courtesy, for Lerma's influence over the King was well-known and, early in his reign, King Philip had notified all his ministers that any order bearing the Duke of Lerma's signature was to be obeyed in the same manner as those which were signed by the King himself. However, all accounts agree that the King's favourite and leader of the government did not use his position of power as much for the benefit of his country as for his own personal gain, and it is estimated that during his years in office he amassed a fortune of forty-four million ducats, much of it at the expense of the state. He was extremely unpopular in Spain where many insulting verses directed against him were circulated; nevertheless, until 1618 he remained in favour with Philip III. It was unfortunate for O Neill that, when he most needed the active support of Spain, the reigning monarch was a weak king under the influence of a man such as Lerma.

O Neill's envoy, Matthew Tully, had been in Madrid for over a year when, in the autumn of 1609, he was joined by Archbishop Conry and Colonel Henry O Neill, but, despite their combined efforts at the Spanish court and O Neill's urgent letters from Rome, months passed and King Philip took no further steps towards O Neill's reconciliation with the King of England. Finally, on 24 January 1610, the Spanish King wrote to his ambassador in Rome:

The Archbishop of Tuam who, as you know, came here on behalf of the Earl of Tiron, has given me a memorial and a letter from the said Earl. I send you a copy of these so that you know their contents, and you will answer him on my behalf as follows:

His labours and sufferings for the catholic cause are very much in my mind and also the good will he has always shown in my service. I have the greatest esteem for his person and desire in the extreme to see him restored with peace and honour *to his country and his lands. I shall endeavour to obtain this when the state of affairs permits it and, the better to achieve his objective, let him also endeavour to obtain help from the Pope. Apart from answering the Earl in this manner and adding anything that may seem suitable to encourage him and keep him in hope, I wish you to represent to His Holiness the good reasons there are that he should favour, help and assist the Earl, and how proper it would be for His Holiness to do so, for the said Earl shows such zeal and has lost much for the faith. I shall be well pleased that you make efforts to this end and that you advise me of what results they may have.*

In the meantime, however, rumours of O Neill's return effectively suspended the movement of Scots and English 'undertakers', or planters, who had been invited by King James to settle on the confiscated lands of the Earls and their followers. From Dublin Castle, in April 1609, Chichester wrote to Salisbury: 'This rumour of Tyrone's return has somewhat cooled men's affections to the Ulster plantation.' The King's Archbishop of Armagh was in favour of deferring the plantation because, he argued: 'There is a common report in England and a strong expectation in Ireland that the Earl of Tyrone or his sons will draw certain forces into Ulster this summer, which is no small discouragement of the plantation.' In fact it was not until 1610 that the plantation was put into effect and, meanwhile, Chichester directed his attention to the problem of 'idle swordmen' who had withdrawn to the woods and boglands and who might cause difficulties for those who came to settle on the lands of the dispossessed. It was feared also that these swordmen would rally to O Neill's support, should he find the means of returning to Ireland, and the Solicitor General, Sir Robert Jacob, pointed out:

There are great probabilities that all the people of that province [Ulster] *would easily run into rebellion if Tyrone should return, or if any munition or aid should be sent to them from foreign parts: for they are all generally diseased with the rumour of the new plantation that is intended, not so much for the manner of it, as because they are afraid to be supplanted or mastered by the English, for though in their* [the State's] *view all the land be in the King's hands, yet the Irish deny this, and claim it is their own inheritance . . . They want no men, notwithstanding the late wars, the famine and the great plague that was amongst them; for ther are 5,000 booked in Tyrone and Coleraine, 4,000 in Armagh, 6,000 in Tyrconnel, and in other counties 3,000, in others 4,000, so that in all that province there are at least 20,000 men of the sword.*

The government's solution to the problem was to have as many as possible of these men transported out of the country to serve in foreign armies. By 1614 Chichester was able to claim that he had sent away 6,000 swordmen to the wars in Sweden. In the year 1609 alone, according to O Neill, 1,200 soldiers, vassals of his, were sent to serve the King of Sweden against the King of Poland. The fate of some of these men is described in a

letter of February 1613, written at O Neill's request by the Spanish
ambassador in Rome to Philip III:

> The Earl of Tiron has told me that, since he left the kingdom of Ireland and
> fled to these parts, the English who appropriated his lands and estates have also
> persecuted his vassals particularly those who followed him in the wars of
> Ireland. Under pain of death they were forced by the English to go to various
> foreign lands and kingdoms to serve in the armies of heretics. In this manner,
> during the year following the Earl's flight from the kingdom of Ireland, the
> English forcibly sent, like slaves, as many as one thousand two hundred soldiers
> to serve the heretics of Moscow and Sweden in their wars against the King of
> Poland. During a battle against the King, seven companies of Irish in the service
> of the heretics passed over to the catholic army. In reprisal for this, the heretics
> killed two other companies of Irish who had been left in garrison, among whom,
> and also among those who are still living, are nephews and close relatives of the
> Earl.
>
> The seven companies who escaped served the King of Poland for three
> years until recently, when he dismissed them without paying them anything for
> their services. As a result of this, the poor men go begging from door to door and
> many of them have come to the Earl for they feel that he has an obligation
> towards them; this is true for, in his cause, they were exiled. The hardship they
> suffer is a cause of great sorrow to the Earl, all the more as he knows that, if they
> return to their country, all of them will be beheaded. Although they are men of
> great courage and would be most faithful to the service of Your Majesty, the
> Archduke Alberto refuses to have them enlisted as soldiers among those of their
> nation who serve Your Majesty in the States of Flanders. I beg Your Majesty to
> order that their case be examined for, if there is need of soldiers in those parts, the
> Earl affirms that none better could be found.

In June 1609, the Marqués de Aytona, Spanish ambassador in Rome,
had been recalled and was replaced by Don Francisco Ruiz de Castro,
Conde de Castro and Duke of Taurisano. Castro was a nephew of the
Duke of Lerma, but this relationship does not seem to have been of any
particular advantage to him. It may perhaps be taken as an indication of the
difference in their characters that, while Lerma, when he lost the King's
favour, managed to have himself created Cardinal in order to avoid
prosecution for misappropriation of funds, his nephew renounced all his
worldly goods and family titles including that of Conde de Lemos which
he had inherited from his elder brother, and ended his days as a Benedictine
monk.

Within three months of the Conde de Castro's arrival, O Neill's eldest
son, Hugh, Baron of Dungannon, died in Rome at the age of twenty-three.
He was buried on 24 September 1609 beside his two uncles, Ruairí and
Cathbharr O Donnell, in the Spanish Franciscan church of San Pietro in
Montorio. Ó Cianáin records that, at the time of Ruairí O Donnell's illness

and death in July of the previous year, the Baron also had fallen ill and 'was a full half year lying in deadly peril and danger of death.' He recovered eventually but his health must have been seriously affected. The Irish chronicler gives no details of the Baron's last illness. His account of events ends in November 1608, but he added to his manuscript a few sad lines lamenting the death of the son of O Neill:

> *Bitter woe! . . . yesterday, the twenty-fourth of September, 1609, the son and proper worthy heir of Ó Néill, Aodh Ó Néill, Baron of Dún Geanainn, he who would have been lord of Cenél Eoghain and the northern half of Ireland without contention or opposition, was buried.*

On his own initiative, the Conde de Castro contributed four hundred crowns towards the expenses of the funeral and wrote the following diplomatic letter to the secretary of the Spanish Council of State, Andrés de Prada:

> *Within the last few days the eldest son of the Earl of Tiron has died here. Having considered that, when the Earl of Tirconel died, the Marques de Aytona gave his sister 300 crowns and that this occasion was of more considerable moment than the other, I took it upon myself to send the Earl of Tiron 400 crowns towards the expenses of the funeral on behalf of His Majesty, for it seemed proper to do this and I believed it would please His Majesty. I have wished to advise you of this so that, at an opportune time, you acquaint His Majesty of it and let me know in what manner it is received for, should it not receive approval, I shall pay the amount from my private income. May God keep you as I wish. Rome, 13 October 1609.*

> *El Conde de Castro.*

Three months later the ambassador received a letter signifying the King's approval of the measures he had taken with regard to the funeral of the Baron of Dungannon. Meanwhile in Madrid O Neill's envoys were doing their utmost to obtain from King Philip and his ministers that prompt action be taken towards averting the confiscation of his lands and of those of the young Earl of Tyrconnell. From Rome, O Neill supported the efforts of his representatives with letters and memorials. On 15 April 1610, King Philip wrote to Castro referring to a recent memorial of O Neill's which Castro had forwarded to the secretary of the Spanish Council of State:

> *I have seen the memorial which was given to you on behalf of the Earl of Tiron and which you forwarded to the secretary Andres de Prada. This memorial has received consideration and it appears that it would be well to give permission to the Earl to seek reconciliation with the King of Great Britain as the Earl seems to wish, for it is not the time to consider any other possibility. You may tell him this and that I shall always have the greatest interest in his person and in*

*anything that may concern him. Tell him also I shall order that he be paid all
that is owed to him so that he may remedy his position and provide for his needs.
You will advise me of the Earl's answer and of your opinion on the matter.*

Yo el Rey.

This brief and casual response suggested indifference to, or lack of
understanding of the deterioration of O Neill's situation, brought about,
as the Earl pointed out repeatedly, by the timorous attitude of King Philip
towards the King of England. Castro, however, who had personal contact
with O Neill, understood the urgency of the situation and, judging by the
date of his reply, it is clear that he lost no time in discussing the King's letter
with O Neill and in dispatching his answer, to which he added his own
personal plea:

*Señor, I have spoken to the Earl of Tiron as Your Majesty ordered by letter of
the 15th of last month. He answered me, with all gratitude to Your Majesty,
that since the only means of regaining his lands is by reconciliation with the King
of England and since he alone cannot obtain this, he begs Your Majesty to
intervene with that King that he may agree to it in accordance with the articles
which the Earl has already sent you.*

*There are so many reasons to move Your Majesty in favour of this noble
gentleman that I myself beg Your Majesty most humbly to order, unless there be
grave reasons against it, that he should be granted his request and as soon as
possible for the Earl says that when the heretics have taken possession of his
lands it will be impossible for him to regain them. May God keep the catholic
person of Your Majesty for the benefit of christendom. Rome, 13th of May
1610.*

El Conde de Castro.

It is evident from Castro's correspondence that he had the greatest
admiration for O Neill and, during the years of his embassy at Rome, he
lost no opportunity of using his influence to support the Earl. It is interesting to note that the ambassador chose to direct his appeals not to his uncle
the Duke of Lerma, but to the secretary of the Council of State, Andrés de
Prada. Prada had been secretary to Philip II's famed half brother, Don Juan
of Austria, and had remained with him during the latter's governorship of
Flanders until his death in 1578. Philip II appointed Prada secretary of the
Council of War in 1586 and he was secretary of Philip III's Council of State
since 1600. He was a man of great experience and his judgement is said to
have carried weight at the council meetings; unfortunately for O Neill, to
whom his support could have been of great assistance, he died in 1611.

At the request of Castro, who shrank from passing on to the Earl yet
another non-commital reply from King Philip, Prada intervened with the
King and obtained that a clear answer and a detailed explanation be sent
to O Neill's repeated letters and memorials. From the palace of Lerma,

near Burgos, where the King was being entertained by the Duke of Lerma, Philip wrote to Castro:

From what you wrote to the secretary Andres de Prada, I have understood the reason for which you have postponed the reply I ordered you to give to the Earl of Tiron and it seems to me that your reason was well considered. You will tell him how much I esteem his person, how much I sympathise with his troubles and how much I wish to see him reinstated.

To endeavour to obtain this by force would be a rash undertaking for there are such great difficulties and inconveniences in the way. In the first place it would be necessary to break the peace with the King of Great Britain and to forego the word which I gave him without his having given me any just motive for doing so. To wage war in the name of the Pope would not be enough to convince the King of Great Britain that the forces used were not mine for it is well known that His Holiness would not undertake such an expedition at his own expense.

In the second place this would be a very costly and difficult war for me at a time when many enemies are ready to attack. These would then be joined by the King of Great Britain whose brother-in-law, the King of Denmark, would then be joined by the heretics of Germany and by the rebels of Flanders. Therefore, the means by which the Earl of Tiron hopes to win would in the end cause his ruin and our loss of prestige.

In the third place the present treasury would not be sufficient for the enormous expense which would be necessary.

These reasons are undeniable and leave no room for doubt and it would not be kindness on my part to undertake a matter of which the issue is so uncertain.

With regard to the alternative of procuring a reconciliation with the King of Great Britain, you can assure the Earl that, before the ambassador Don Pedro de Çuñiga left Spain, I charged him most pressingly to use all possible means to obtain on my behalf that the Earl be reinstated and restored to favour. I repeated this in writing to him when he was in England and he always answered that he could discern no inclinations towards this in the King of England and, in order to avoid further harm to the Earl, it was necessary to await a favourable opportunity. I gave the same order to Don Alonso de Velasco who succeeded to Don Pedro de Çuñiga and charged him also to procure for the Earl by all possible means a reconciliation with the King and the restitution of his lands.

You shall be kept advised so that you may inform the Earl of any developments. In the meantime the Earl must prudently moderate his feelings and preserve his life and some day by some means or other it will please God that he attain his aim. Let him rest assured that I do not wish it any less than himself. For your part you shall console and encourage him and you shall let me know what results this may have and what are your opinions. Lerma, 2nd of June 1610.

Yo el Rey.

In Madrid, during the same month of June 1610, Matthew Tully submitted a memorial to King Philip on behalf of Archbishop Conry. On 10 July the memorial was discussed at a meeting of the Council of State whose recommendations to the King were as follows:

> The Irishman Mateo Tulió, agent in this city for the Earl of Tiron, states in a memorial which Your Majesty referred to this Council that Fray Florencio Conrio, Archbishop of Tuam, came to this court nine months ago on behalf of the Earl of Tiron and of the Irish catholics by order of His Holiness and of the said Earl. The Archbishop has served Your Majesty for the past twelve years since the last war of Ireland, helping the Earls O Neill and O Donnell whom he has always encouraged to remain firm, as they have done, in the service of God and of Your Majesty. Later he came to Spain whence Your Majesty sent him to the said catholics with messages of importance. On his return here Your Majesty was pleased to employ him in other matters of great consequence. He is a man who can give great service in anything that concerns Ireland and, as the catholics of that kingdom have great respect for him and confidence in him, he can keep them firm in their good dispositions.
>
> The Archbishop is now in such straitened circumstances that he cannot appear in public with the propriety required by the dignity of his calling. For this reason he is resolved to return to his country where nothing but death can be his fate. Should he leave without having obtained a settlement of the affairs of the Earl of Tiron and of the other catholics of Ireland, they would all despair of ever receiving this favour from Your Majesty.
>
> Mateo Tulio humbly begs Your Majesty, in consideration of what is stated above, to order that the Archbishop be granted an allowance in keeping with his dignity and his services while he is engaged in matters which are of such consequence to the service of God and of Your Majesty.
>
> It is the opinion of the Council that this Archbishop is a man of good life and exemplary virtue and that his presence is necessary in this court for dealing with matters which concern his nation and because it is important to have his advice. Therefore it seems that he could be granted an allowance of fifty or sixty ducats a month so that he may continue his services with some decorum and in keeping with the dignity of his office. Let this be ordered according to Your Majesty's pleasure. Madrid, 10th of July 1610.

It seems unlikely that the Archbishop was seriously considering leaving Spain in the summer of 1610 at a time when his presence there could be of considerable assistance to O Neill. Perhaps Matthew Tully, with his experience of bureaucratic delays, was merely using an argument which he hoped would be effective; in fact, as a result of his memorial, the Archbishop was granted fifty ducats a month and remained in Madrid to continue his work for the Irish catholic cause.

Shortly after his successful appeal on behalf of Archbishop Conry, Matthew Tully was arrested and imprisoned on a charge of bigamy. The charge was false, and it is very likely that he was the victim of an attempt by English agents to remove him from a position of influence. I have found no evidence to support this theory, but several mentions of him in the English State Papers indicate quite clearly that he was regarded as a 'dangerous man' by the ministers of King James, whose ambassador in Madrid had vowed to 'keep a vigilant eye' upon Matthew Tully. At any rate, on the 17 July 1610, from his prison in Madrid, Matthew sent the following memorial to King Philip:

> *Señor, Mateo Tulio, agent in this city for the Earl of Tiron, declares that both he and his wife were accused before the judges of being married twice, for which they were arrested and are imprisoned in the city jail. This matter has already been before the Council of State. It was referred to Don Diego Brochero who found that all the accusations made against the petitioner and his wife consisted of calumnies and lies. Consequently, he declared them not guilty and free. Nevertheless, their opponents filed a complaint before the judges of the court. Another enquiry was carried out and it was found that the petitioner and his wife were not guilty of any offence. Despite this, without an order from Your Majesty, no one will set them free. Therefore, the petitioner humbly begs that, on behalf of Your Majesty, Don Diego Brochero should order the judges to release them, at least on bail, because the petitioner is ill and his wife is pregnant and within days of giving birth. Besides, this case has already been heard and cleared by Don Diego Brochero.*

Both Matthew and his wife, Elena Fitzgerald, were in fact married twice. However, Elena's first husband was dead before her second marriage and so, presumably, was Matthew's first wife. The matter was referred to an official of the court, Don Fernando Mena de Barrnuevo, who reported a week later:

> *This gentleman and his wife have now been set free. I have dealt with the matter privately because if I followed the usual legal procedures, we should never get to the end of it.*

After his release, Matthew wrote to O Neill what must have been a very interesting letter. Unfortunately, we have no means of knowing its contents. The only reference to it is to be found in a report of December 1610 from the Council of State to King Philip:

> *In a letter of the 30th of September last, the Earl of Tiron states that Matheo Tulio, his agent in this court, has written to him that there is little need for his presence here since the Archbishop of Tuam is here also and may attend with more safety to his affairs and to those of the kingdom of Ireland. Therefore, the Earl begs Your Majesty to transfer to San Sebastian the allowance which the said Matheo Tulio receives in this court, so that from there he may be in a better position to correspond with the catholics of Ireland, with the Archbishop and with the Earl.*

But Matthew did not leave Madrid. His health was seriously affected by his term of imprisonment and he died in that city in the spring of 1611. In Rome, O Neill must have mourned the death of this staunch supporter of his. There is little doubt that Matthew Tully was the principal co-ordinator of the Earls' escape from Ireland in September 1607. This is borne out by a letter of the Vicar General of the diocese of Killaloe, Dr Donal O Carroll, who, writing from Rome on 10 November 1607, asked to be heartily commended to 'Matthew Tullie unto whom all our country is bound for ever for this his attempt.'

CHAPTER SIX

'Feigned Friendship'

They [the English] *themselves . . . teach us this manner of feigned friendship and of destruction by peace.*

O Neill to Andrés Velázquez, 23 May 1615.

Meanwhile, King Philip's letter of June 1610 had reached his ambassador in Rome and its contents were made known to O Neill. Philip's explanation of his attitude did not have the desired effect of causing O Neill to 'moderate his feelings' and, with the restraining hand of Archbishop Conry no longer upon him, O Neill promptly replied in unequivocal and accusing terms. In a memorial dated 29 July, he reminds the King of the many letters which in past years he and his father, Philip II, sent to Ireland, urging O Neill to continue the war when England was then offering good terms of peace. At the King's request he has, since his escape from Ireland, many times informed him of the circumstances and asked for a decision. Two and a half years passed without any reply from the King, yet, during that time, the Spanish ambassadors in Flanders and in Italy were assuring O Neill that the King had promised to send a favourable reply very soon and were asking him to be patient. Now, after two and a half years of silence, Philip's answer is merely his permission for O Neill to seek reconciliation with the King of England. Philip's long delay has caused further deterioration in O Neill's position and it is not now possible for him to obtain satisfactory terms of reconciliation through his efforts alone. In conclusion, he declares that, in conscience and justice, King Philip has the obligation of procuring from the King of England the restoration of his estates and his return to favour. In addition, he has three further requests: firstly, that he be allowed to go either to Flanders or to Galicia where he will be nearer to the seat of negotiations and in a better position to deal with possible difficulties. Secondly, he asks that John Bathe be permitted to go to the Spanish ambassador in London for the purpose of assisting in the negotiations. Thirdly, he asks that, in order to avoid delays, the answer to his memorial be given in Madrid to his son Colonel Henry O Neill and to the Archbishop of Tuam.

When King Philip and his Council of State had considered this memorial, it was decided that an account of it be sent to the ambassador in London, Don Alonso de Velasco, asking him to take what steps he might deem most appropriate, but the Council of State remained firm in the opinion that O Neill should not leave Rome until such a time as he might do so in safety. His request that Don Juan Batheo, or John Bathe, be allowed to go to London to assist in the negotiations appears to have been denied, for Bathe remained in Madrid. However, the fact that O Neill had named him for a mission of such importance was a strong recommendation.

John Bathe was employed by the Spanish government in delicate matters of great secrecy which, according to a report of Andrés Velázquez, the Councillor in charge of the secret service, he discharged faithfully and well, and he was given a salary of forty crowns a month. He was a brother of the famous Jesuit, William Bathe, and it was in their family home at Drumcondra that O Neill had married Mabel Bagenal in 1591, thereby making a mortal enemy of the bride's brother, Marshal Henry Bagenal, commander of Queen Elizabeth's army in Ireland.

After the accession of James I, John Bathe came to be recognised as a spokesman for the Anglo-Irish catholics of the Pale. He appears to have moved with equal ease in London and at the court of Spain; he had a pension from King Philip and became equerry of King James. He was in close touch with members of the English Privy Council and also with the Spanish ambassador in London and, by 1624, the Spanish Council of State were convinced that he was a double agent. The Irish in Spain had come to that conclusion much earlier. On 12 April 1618 the Archbishop of Tuam, Florence Conry, who was then about to leave Madrid for Flanders, wrote to King Philip explaining his suspicions of Bathe:

All those of my nation are under strong obligation to serve Your Majesty because of the royal protection and favours extended to them, and particularly to myself whom Your Majesty has always trusted with the important affairs of that nation. Therefore, before setting out on my journey to Flanders, I feel obliged to give adequate information to Your Majesty concerning a certain person of my nation who may in time do serious disservice to Your Majesty, if the royal councillors are not forewarned and put on their guard.

In this court there resides an Irishman named Don Juan Batheo to whom Your Majesty gives forty crowns a month, not in consideration of his own services to Your Majesty, nor of those of his ancestors, all of whom served the Crown of England, for they are of English race, but because of his good parts and particularly because of what he calls his art of memory.

I have learned from a secret and reliable source that, when the said Don Juan first came here, he promised the then Viceroy of Ireland, called Arthuro Cicester, to inform him of affairs of state which he might hear and find out in this court and which would be of service to the King of England and, to confirm his loyalty to the said Viceroy, when the said Don Juan landed in Lisbon, he sent back certain information concerning the navy . . .

At first I thought that he would not give information of importance and that, although he had given that promise, it was only to comply with the demands of the English and so that his family, who are well regarded by them, should not come under suspicion on his account . . . But last year, he went to Ireland. Don Juan Digby, previously ambassador of England here, told an Irishman that he was very angry with Don Juan Batheo because he did not visit him when he was here and he said that Don Juan would pay for his discourtesy if ever he returned to Ireland. But when, as I say, he was in Ireland last year, not only did he come to no harm at all, but on the contrary, during his visit which lasted many months, the Viceroy and all the councillors treated him with honour and, any time he wished, he had meals at the table of the Viceroy, of the chancellor and of the other councillors.

When he returned to Madrid, some Irish people told him they were surprised the English did not trouble and harass him as they usually do in the case of other Irishmen arriving from Spain, especially as the ambassador Digby was annoyed with him (as it was believed) and must have been aware of his arrival.

He replied that, although he had dealings with those ministers during most of his time in Ireland, about twenty days or a month before he left that country, he went into hiding in his mother's house for fear of those same ministers. But it is known here by a person of repute that such was not the case and that he left Ireland with permission from the Viceroy.

I send this account so that Your Majesty may see clearly the grounds for suspicion against this person . . . The said Don Juan is a very clever and astute man of great intelligence, and for that reason I believe it is dangerous that he should be at the court . . . Your Majesty could order that he join the company of Irish soldiers serving in the navy where, I believe, he will be removed from the possibility of causing damage. In order to hide the purpose of this business, Your Majesty could issue a general order that no Irish should receive payments of salary or allowances at the court and that all those who are here should go to serve in the navy. If the said Don Juan should not wish to go, as I expect, Your Majesty could then with justice stop his salary.

I solemnly declare that I do not wish him any harm and that I would never have spoken of this matter if I did not fear that, not to do so, would be to the disservice of Your Majesty, of God and of my nation. God knows that it goes to my heart to have to uncover the faults of another, although it be to avoid a greater evil. May God keep Your Majesty for the good of all Christendom and especially the afflicted catholics of Ireland. From my lodgings, 12th of April 1612.

Your Majesty's chaplain and servant,

Fray Florencio, Conryo,
Archbishop of Tuam.'

The Archbishop's letter was discussed at a meeting of the Council of State on 19 May 1612, when it was recommended that Bathe should no longer be trusted or admitted to the court. However, no action had yet been taken in that regard when, on 16 July, following an argument and a sword-fight with the historian, Philip O Sullivan, John Bathe stabbed and killed Donal O Sullivan Beare who had come upon the scene. After this event, Archbishop Conry's letter was retrieved from the files of the Council of State and the following note was added to it:

> *With what has happened on the 16th* [of July 1618] *this matter takes on a different complexion. If the Church protects him* [John Bathe] *he could be banished from all the dominions of His Majesty. Those who are dealing with his case should be notified accordingly.*

As yet I have been unsuccessful in my search for the legal records of the case, but from Philip O Sullivan's account of the event, it is evident that O Sullivan Beare's death was no accident. In the closing chapters of his work, published in 1621, the historian records the unfortunate events of the year 1618; he refers to O Cahan's death in the Tower of London, to the sea-battle of July 2nd of the Spanish fleet against the Turks, in which, although the Spaniards were victorious, six young Irish noblemen lost their lives, and he continues:

> *But the final stroke of evil fortune was that on the 16th of that same month, O Sullivan, Chieftain of Beare, in whom the Irish had then their greatest hope, perished lamentably in this way.*
>
> *John Bathe, an Anglo-Irishman, was so favoured by O Sullivan that he benefited greatly by his influence and patronage. He was treated as such a great friend that he was even received into his home and invited to his table; but, with total disregard for such favours, John acted with effrontery when a trivial argument arose over money given to him by O Sullivan. This behaviour in no way enhanced the noble lineage of such a great man, or his reputation among the Irish, or among the English from whom he is descended.*
>
> *Philip, the author of this history, and O Sullivan's cousin, was angered by this behaviour and remonstrated with John. Consequently, near the monastery of St. Dominic in Madrid, they attacked each other with drawn swords. From the beginning of the fight, John was struck by such overwhelming fear that, uttering loud cries, he constantly gave ground and Philip wounded him in the face with a sword thrust; he would have killed him, had not Edmund O Moore and Gerald MacMorris, sent by O Sullivan, and two Spanish knights, protected him, and had not Philip himself been arrested by an official of the law.*
>
> *A crowd then gathered from all sides and, among others, came O Sullivan, carrying a rosary in his left hand and gloves in his right hand. John, observing him off his guard, unaware of danger and looking in the opposite direction, made his way up to him through the crowd and, stabbing him through the left upper arm, and again striking him in the throat, killed him.*

Philip, struggling with the official of the law, escaped and hid himself in the house of the ambassador of France, the Marquis Seneccia. John was thrown into prison together with his relative, Francis Bathe, and O Driscoll, Philip's kinsman, who were present at the fight.

O Sullivan's funeral ceremonies took place in that monastery on the following day in the presence of a large assembly of Spanish nobles, and the expenses were paid through the good offices of the illustrious knight and royal councillor, Don Diego Brochero.

At the time of his death, O Sullivan was 57 years of age. He was a man of great benevolence and generosity, especially towards the poor and needy. It was his custom to attend two or three masses daily, praying with great fervour to God and the saints. Often, having done penance for his sins, he received the Most Holy Body of the Lord. His sudden and unfortunate death was very much out of keeping with his life; on that very day he was present at two masses and, when he was wounded, he was absolved of his sins by the priests. In stature he was tall and elegant, with a handsome face, and he grew old with dignity.

From this account of Philip O Sullivan's sword–fight with Bathe, it would appear that it was a regular duel, with O Moore and MacMorris possibly filling the role of Philip's seconds and the two Spanish knights acting for Bathe. However, as one might expect, Bathe's account is quite different; two years later, in a memorial of 17 September 1620, he had occasion to refer to his fight with Philip O Sullivan. It is not clear whether or not he had spent the intervening years in prison but it is obvious that he realised it would have been impossible for him to continue living in Spain. He addressed his memorial to King Philip:

Don Juan Batheo declares that, some time ago, he begged Your Majesty to order that the salary of forty crowns a month which he has been receiving in this court for the past ten years be transferred to Naples so that he may receive it there near the person of the Viceroy.

The petitioner attributes to some sinister report the fact that this favour has not yet been granted, for it is well known that, when he was making his way directly to the palace, as he did every day at the same time, without any thought of trouble and without carrying weapons of any sort, except for his sword, he was attacked by the nephew of the Earl of Birhaven, by the Earl's majordomo, by the Earl himself, and by two Irish soldiers, as well as the Earl's lackey, his page and others, so that he would have been cut to pieces were it not that some Spanish knights took pity on him and came to his aid, although they did not know him and he had never seen them before.

These facts are made clear by the investigation carried out on the spot by the magistrate and his officials. So that Your Majesty may be informed of the truth, the petitioner humbly begs that an order be sent to the magistrate and his officials and to the relevant notary, to give a full account of the facts and Your Majesty will then see the truth of the case. If it is not as stated by the petitioner, let Your

Majesty order that he be beheaded, but he expects that, finding it true, Your Majesty will, with customary generosity, grant him favour.

Although this account is the undeniable truth, the petitioner cannot find anyone to advise him and to appear at the prison before the local judge, for he has no money to give to legal advisers, solicitors, procurators, notaries, or to anyone else, since he lacks even the necessary funds for his own maintenance, and, in these circumstances, even were he more innocent than an angel, he would not receive justice, and so he begs Your Majesty to protect him.

However, Philip O Sullivan and his friends believed that the chieftain's death was no accident and that, as Archbishop Conry had warned, Bathe was an agent in the pay of England. It is certain that O Sullivan Beare was at that time planning to lead a rising in Ireland. A letter sent to him from Berehaven by an Irish priest called Tadeo Huolano leaves no doubt as to his plans. The letter is written in English and is dated 18 September 1618, when Father Huolano was still unaware of the chieftain's death:

My duty remembered unto your right honourable Lordship . . . It was God's will after enduring many crosses that I have arrived safely unto this country, and then being greatly persecuted I was constrained to recollect myself within the confines of rocks and islands . . . At length I could come with much ado to speak with your friends, acquainting of your intention and purpose.

And first your honour may understand in what perplexity and necessity your friends are. All the lords are in danger to lose their lands, the cities their liberty, the poor men their money and chattels and, not content with this, unless they renounce their faith, they must take a banishment out of the whole realm: so being without refuge that it is pity to see them. And let your honour be sure that all, both spiritual and temporal, both cities and country men, are so willing and ready to concur with the matter and arise with good courage and free will . . . But they are slow in beginning any stirring before they see some assistance, being already many times deceived, and specially the chiefest of the country, in hoping to have succour; but for all that they have such confidence in your fidelity and discretion that, if they had seen you once landed, they should all take your part and help you to follow your purpose. I have tried some of the chiefest in Munster worthy to be heard, and many of the citizens in whom I trust. Also they cast a plot among themselves when you should land here, to destroy and banish all Englishmen and take possession of the cities, towns and fortresses of all the country within eight and forty hours.

I have done also your message in the country of Connaught which is ready to your contentment . . . but none of them will stir until they see yourself in person or your letters, but above all they expect yourself with good succour.

The news of O Sullivan Beare's death must have come as a sad blow to Father Huolano and his friends. As for John Bathe, he was eventually allowed to go free and he took up residence in London where he received from King James an annual pension of £500. At any rate, ten years earlier, in 1610, neither O Neill nor the Spanish authorities entertained any suspicion of him.

Early in the summer of 1610 King Philip and his court left Madrid to spend some time in the province of Burgos, first at Lerma, where the King's favourite had his principal residence, and later at Aranda de Duero. It was at Aranda, during the month of August, that Colonel Henry O Neill, the Earl of Tyrone's eldest surviving son, became ill and died at the age of twenty-three. It was just eleven months since the death of Henry's brother Hugh, Baron of Dungannon. The sad news was conveyed to O Neill by the Conde de Castro to whom the King had written as follows:

> Don Enrique Oneil, eldest son of the Earl of Tiron, died of illness here three days ago. He had come from Flanders where he served me with an infantry regiment of his nation. His death has grieved me, not only because he was the son of his father who will mourn his loss, but also because he had great qualities and served me well, for which I was well pleased with him. I have ordered that he be buried in a manner suited to his rank in a much honoured chapel of the Monastery of St. Francis. I have wished to inform you of this and to order, as I do, that you visit the Earl on my behalf, give him my condolence and tell him, in consolation, that the faith and virtue of his son give good cause for the pious belief that he is on the way to salvation. You will ask the Earl, as coming from yourself, what soldier of nobility and prestige among those of his nation could be called upon to take up the appointment which was held by his son. When you have done this you will advise me of the Earl's reply. Aranda, 28 August 1610.

> *Yo el Rey.*

At least three officers of Colonel Henry's regiment had received permission from the Archduke Albert to travel to Spain with their colonel; they were Captain Jenquin Fitzsimon, Captain Juan Rath and Captain Eugenio O Neill. Fitzsimon was a soldier of long experience who had fought under O Neill in the war in Ireland; Rath had captained the ship in which the Earls of Tyrone and Tyrconnell had escaped from Ireland in 1607, and Eugenio O Neill, Henry's cousin, rose to fame in later years and is better known to us as Eoghan Rua. It is not clear if any of these officers were with their colonel at Aranda; at any rate, shortly before his death, Henry petitioned the King not to allow that the command of his regiment be given to any other than a person nominated by his father, the Earl of Tyrone. Inspired by the same concern for the future of the Irish regiment, Archbishop Florence Conry wrote to King Philip from Madrid on the 9th of September urging the immediate appointment of Captain Eugenio O Neill as colonel of the regiment. He feared, as he explained, that any delay would provide the King of England's ministers with an opportunity of harming the regiment; he believed, moreover, that this would be the Earl of Tyrone's wish, for there was no other suitable person of his blood in Flanders. The King, however, was not to be hurried and made no decision until he was informed by letters from the Conde de Castro:

> *The Earl begs Your Majesty, as a particular favour, to give this post to his*
> *eldest son, Don Juan Onel, with the same salary and terms as were given to his*
> *brother. The Earl says that, although Don Juan is only about twelve years of*
> *age, the affection which all the soldiers had for the late Colonel and the honour*
> *and respect they owe to the Earl, his father, give reason to hope that all will be*
> *well pleased to serve Your Majesty under his command . . . . It is not necessary*
> *on this occasion that I also should beg for this favour which Your Majesty must*
> *grant, all the more as the Earl offers to provide a competent person to act as*
> *lieutenant to his son until he is old enough to be in command of the regiment .*

The King agreed to the appointment of O Neill's son as colonel and, shortly afterwards, also addressed a letter of recommendation to the Archduke Albert in favour of Captain Eugenio O Neill for the post of major of the Irish regiment. However, the Earl had received no answer from Philip to his memorial of 29 July 1610 and on 5 February 1611 the Conde de Castro was moved to write to the secretary of the Council of State, Andrés de Prada:

> *The Earl of Tiron has complained bitterly to me that, although he has written*
> *by every ordinary to His Majesty asking for a clear answer as to what His*
> *Majesty intends to do on his behalf with the King of England, up to the present*
> *he has received no clear reply on this point. This has been the cause of his ruin,*
> *for the King of England has seen what little account His Majesty has made of the*
> *Earl and the delay that has been made in the settlement of his affairs; conse-*
> *quently the English King has given his estates to Englishmen and Scots . . . Had*
> *the Earl believed that this were to happen he would have delivered himself unto*
> *his King rather than come to such a pass. Indeed he is not beyond doing this, or*
> *anything else that may suit him, if there should be any further delay in dealing*
> *with his affairs . . . This nobleman is worthy of compassion. He also told me,*
> *although he asked me afterwards not to repeat this, that, since His Majesty is*
> *pleased to admit to his dominions the Earl of Boduer, Admiral of Scotland,*
> *who is a greater enemy of the King of England, he does not see why he himself*
> *should be refused admission; and certainly he seems to speak with reason. If this*
> *is possible help him to obtain permission to live within the King's territories for*
> *he greatly wishes to do so. But, above all, let them send me orders to tell him the*
> *truth.*

King Philip was not moved; his reply was that O Neill should remain in Rome until advice was received from the ambassador in London, Don Alonso de Velasco. However, the King increased the Earl's grant by one hundred ducats a month and ordered the payment of his debts which amounted to four thousand ducats;   but it should be noted that the money for this payment had not yet been provided a year later when Castro wrote that, as O Neill's creditors were pressing him, he had been obliged to give him six hundred ducats from the funds of the embassy.

Undeterred by disappointments and reverses, O Neill persevered in his efforts to find means of rallying support for an expedition to Ireland. He appealed to the Pope, setting out in a memorial the increasingly difficult position of the catholics in Ireland. In agreement with William Meade, the one-time Recorder of Cork, who had arrived in Rome sent by the catholics of Ireland as their representative, in December 1611, a four-point request was submitted to the Pope and to the King of Spain which consisted of the following articles:

> 1. For the satisfaction of their souls, the catholics of Ireland beg His Holiness to declare, only in secret and by special Bull, that the King of England is a heretic, that all his subjects and vassals are absolved from obedience to him, and that they may unite and take arms against him to free themselves from his tyranny and re-establish and maintain the catholic religion in that kingdom.
> 2. When the catholics have taken all the monasteries and the lands of the churches which the heretics have usurped, they beg His Holiness to allow the prelates of the kingdom to order that the income of the said churches be used for the maintenance of the navy and army which would be raised against the heretics.
> 3. They also ask that His Holiness and His Catholic Majesty be pleased to appoint some general of the said kingdom who will rally the other catholics and direct and govern this Holy League.
> 4. Finally, the said catholics and the Earl of Tiron are aware of the difficulty of having help sent to them openly, therefore they humbly beg, in order to give initial encouragement to the enterprise, that His Holiness send them some financial aid and intercede with His Catholic Majesty to do the same for, until the opportune time, it does not suit that too many people should know of the plans.

The petition had no positive result, for the Pope referred the matter to the King of Spain who declared that this was a religious concern upon which he would make no decision until he was informed of the Pope's wishes, and so the matter rested there. O Neill then appealed to King Philip requesting that, at least, he be allowed to reside in Spain where he would be nearer to his country and better able to correspond with those of his vassals who had remained in Ireland. This also was denied but the Earl continued to watch for any opportunity which might be turned to advantage. When, in March 1612, some months after the death of the Queen of Spain, it was rumoured that Philip was to marry the daughter of James I, the Spanish prelate, Dr Vivas, wrote from Rome on behalf of O Neill asking that favourable conditions for Irish catholics and for the Earl of Tyrone be included in the terms of marriage agreement. This request had no effect for the marriage was never seriously contemplated. Once again O Neill requested to be allowed to reside in Spain, pointing out how harmful the climate of Rome was to the Irish, so many of whom had died since their arrival there four years earlier; he also pointed out that Philip had admitted to his territories other nobles who had fled from their countries and from the King of England, such as the Earl of Bothwell, Admiral of Scotland, and the lord of Berehaven, O Sullivan Beare.   The King answered that the reasons for not granting this request had been pointed out on other occasions. O Neill insisted no further at that time and Castro reported to the King:

> *Señor, I gave the Earl of Tiron Your Majesty's answer to his request for permission to go to Spain, and I assure Your Majesty that he has shown such resignation and obedience that no more could be asked from the most obliged vassal. The Earl is a great nobleman and Your Majesty owes much to his devotion and loyalty.*

In view of the continued efforts made by Philip and his ministers to ensure that O Neill should remain quietly in Rome, it seems strange that in November 1612 the King should write to the Conde de Castro asking him to consult the Earl of Tyrone with regard to the possibility of a rising in Scotland, its chances of success and the help which might be required. Castro discussed the matter with O Neill and sent a full account of the views of the Earl; he also reported on the opinions of William Meade who had returned from Scotland a few months earlier, and on the support which might be expected from the Pope in the event of a rising in that country.

O Neill must have wondered at the reason for this apparent change in attitude of King Philip and his ministers who now asked for his views which he had sent to them many times previously and which they had repeatedly ignored. Nevertheless he wrote yet another memorial which was forwarded with the ambassador's letter and in which he gave his views on the situation in Ireland and in England; he reminded the King of the saying common even among Englishmen that whoever wishes to conquer England must first begin with Ireland; but he was ready, he added, if such were the King's wishes, to lead an attack on England, knowing that this would be immediately supported by risings in both Ireland and Scotland. He declared that the conquest would be relatively easy, but only, he stressed, provided that prompt action and the element of surprise were ensured. When these documents had been examined by the Council of State, the recommendation to the King was that they be set aside to await a better opportunity and that an acknowledgement be sent to Castro saying that the matter was being considered. King Philip's decision was: *omit the reply*.

The attitude of the Spanish government appeared to be consistently in favour of upholding the peace treaty with England, yet English fears of an expedition to Ireland, led by O Neill, were never completely laid to rest.

This had been reported to King Philip by successive ambassadors in London, one of whom had remarked in colourful terms: 'To the English, he is a bridle. Their fear of him gnaws at their entrails.' Expectations of his return had delayed the Ulster Plantation and had encouraged his supporters in Ireland in their resistance to the authority of the English government. Consequently King James and his ministers had given some thought to the possibility of contriving O Neill's peaceful return on conditions that would be acceptable to them. Various tentative moves had been made on both sides, with O Neill constantly and wisely attempting to involve King Philip as mediator and guarantor of any eventual agreement. Nothing had come of these moves, perhaps because of Philip's inertia or unwillingness; the success of such negotiations would have depended largely on their timing, for King James' inclination towards them varied according to changes of the situation in Ireland.

In 1613, new and more serious approaches were made to O Neill on behalf of King James. It was a time of growing unrest in Ireland. Much resentment had been caused by Chichester's uncompromising policy towards the catholics of the cities and of the Pale, by the imprisonment and the savage public execution of the eighty-year-old Bishop of Down and Connor, Cornelius O Devaney, and by the creation of new boroughs to procure an artificial majority of protestants in the Dublin parliament. In England, Salisbury had died the previous year and the young Scotsman, Robert Carr, had become the notorious favourite of James I who had created him Viscount Rochester in 1611.

In the early summer of 1613 O Neill in Rome received a letter from Father Hugh Mac Caughwell, the Franciscan who had been tutor to his two eldest sons and who was now Guardian of the Irish Franciscan monastery in Louvain. The facts which appear from this letter and from the accompanying documents are that Viscount Rochester sent an agent to Flanders for the purpose of finding out, on behalf of King James, what would be O Neill's proposals for a reconciliation, and this English agent had an interview with Father Mac Caughwell.

It is interesting to note that Rochester was then about to be married to a member of the Howard family. It was during 1613 that his liaison with the wife of the young Earl of Essex, Frances Howard, daughter of the Earl of Suffolk, led her to seek an annulment of her marriage to Essex. The hearing of her case, on grounds of her husband's impotence, caused somewhat of a scandal but the annulment was granted and, with the approval of King James, she was married to Rochester in September of that year and, in November, her new bridegroom was created Earl of Somerset. It is not unlikely that O Neill's friends among the Howards, perhaps Northampton, may have used Rochester's influence with the King at a time when James' favourite was in need of the Howards' support. At any rate, Father Mac Caughwell's letter to O Neill, whom he addresses as

'Your Excellency', describes his interview with Rochester's agent, to whom he refers as 'this English gentleman'. It should be noted, of course, that the original of this letter, which O Neill would have kept in his possession, was certainly not in Spanish, which is the language of the version preserved in the archives of Simancas and of which the following is a translation:

After some conversation he [this English gentleman] *asked me to write to Your Excellency begging you to state in a personal letter what are your claims from the King of England concerning your estates. I told him that Your Excellency would have nothing to do with such a matter without first being assured that the King would accept your demands. He answered me that it was against the honour and reputation of His Majesty to open negotiations and offer reconciliation to any of his subjects and that it would be great arrogance on the part of the subject to await an initial offer from his King as regards reconciliation, which I could not deny.*

In the end he showed me a letter from Roberto Caari, Viscount Racester, Commander of the order of the Golden Fleece, and one of the principal Privy Councillors of His Majesty. This letter was written in the name of His Majesty and was given to this man, as he is trusted to deal with Your Excellency of its contents with greater secrecy than any other. Consequently His Majesty gave him power and authority to negotiate with Your Excellency on all points concerning this matter and he was asked to inform His Majesty with all possible promptitude of the answer and intentions of Your Excellency. This man wished to know from me what you claimed from His Majesty or what settlement you wished to come to with him. He swore and protested many times that he himself would do everything possible to help Your Excellency in your claims but he begs you not to ask His Majesty for anything that is not reasonable considering that you have not now as much power to warrant the insistence on punctilio with His Majesty as, sword in hand, you had in the past with the Queen of England when you were not treated according to your pleasure. I told him that Your Excellency was never more powerful than at present for now the justice of your cause is manifest to all the world, that you had never offended His Majesty since the time of your reconciliation, and that all you had done was to flee for your life without his permission from the outrages which the Viceroy of Ireland inflicted upon you.

Finally, after lengthy discussion, he wishes that you send all your claims in writing to His Majesty with all possible humility, and that you appoint one of your vassals to negotiate this matter with His Majesty. He says that the person appointed by Your Excellency will have full and free access to the Court of London, and that he will be free to leave it and to deal with all things concerning the expediting of this matter.

This man awaits the reply of Your Excellency within forty days from the date of this letter. On behalf of His Majesty he promises that the terms of agreement will not be so rigorous as they were when in your hand you held a naked sword, for the King will give you either your own lands, or the equivalent, or even better lands.

I told him that what Your Excellency suffered from most was not the loss of your own estates but the confiscation of the estates of your vassals, titled lords, who are now imprisoned and whose lands are distributed among English and Scots, and that the liberty of these lords would be a great incentive for Your Excellency to submit to His Majesty in all things. I also told him that Your Excellency would rather choose to live and die in exile than to allow the honour of your house to fall into disrepute for the liberty of your vassals.

Finally he told me clearly that His Majesty is much inclined to receive Your Excellency into his favour and that this is the opportunity, and the time is now or never.

He swore to me that no one knows of this matter except His Majesty and the said Roberto who has promised this man that it will not go to the Council but will be settled by private decision of His Majesty. Consequently he wishes Your Excellency to make all possible haste and to write a preliminary letter to him stating some part of your intentions so as to give him some good hope.

I informed His Serene Highness [the Archduke Albert] and the Secretary Mancicidor of this matter and they wish to know the reply of Your Excellency, but you may be assured that, if the King of England knew that the King of Spain or His Highness had any knowledge of this matter, he would have nothing more to do with it and would not give you audience. Therefore it is necessary to use the greatest possible secrecy in dealing with His Catholic Majesty.

On receipt of this document, O Neill consulted with the Spanish ambassador in Rome who forwarded a copy of it to King Philip, together with a letter from O Neill. In his letter, the Earl pointed out that, although from England he was urged to keep the matter secret, in proof of his devotion to the Spanish crown, he was informing Philip of King James' proposals. He declared that he would take no decision and would accept no offer of reconciliation from the King of England unless it were with the approval and on the express order of King Philip, and he asked that, if Philip did not wish to be involved in the negotiations, he himself be given permission to carry these out and to go to Flanders for that purpose. The ambassador, Castro, added his own letter, stressing the urgency of a prompt reply and asking the King to grant O Neill's requests for, he wrote: 'What I assure Your Majesty is that the great faith of the Earl, his zeal, his goodness and his unswerving loyalty and devotion to the Crown of Spain deserve much from Your Majesty.'

It is probable that O Neill would have regarded these approaches with suspicion, for at other times he spoke of the 'feigned friendship' of the English and of their 'playing with both hands'. Nonetheless, it was an opportunity of forcing King Philip to commit himself one way or the other.

On 22 August 1613, the Spanish Council of State met in Madrid and discussed this new turn of events and O Neill's request for permission to go to Flanders. The four Councillors present at this meeting were the elderly and experienced Don Cristóbal de Moura, Marqués de Castel Rodrigo, who had been one of Philip II's principal advisers, the Duque del Infantado, the Marqués de Villafranca and the Marqués de la Laguna. Don Cristóbal's opinion was:

> *In view of present circumstances, the Earl of Tiron should stay where he is; he should be told this for, even if at present the King of England received him well, later, given the slightest opportunity, he would do him an evil turn.*

The advice of the Duque del Infantado was:

> *Your Majesty should take no part whatever in this matter because, if we advise the Earl to go, we should be obliged to help and assist him in any resulting difficulty, which could involve grave inconvenience; and if we persuade him to stay, we should be forced to increase his allowance as previously he requested. The Earl should be told that he himself should examine and consider what decision would be best for him to take and that Your Majesty will rejoice in his success.*

The opinion of the Marqués de Villafranca was recorded as follows:

> *If the Earl went, his life would be in evident danger, and if we keep him where he is, he could be of great importance in the event of the King of England's death and the minority of the King's successor, for the Earl would have great following and support over there and so . . . [he should] be maintained in Rome for this purpose even at the cost of adding something to his allowance . . . God may provide many ways in which to gain great benefit from what expense may be incurred for, perhaps, by adding very little to the number of warships of Flanders and by a quick reinforcement of the army there at an opportune time, together with the help of the Earl and his followers, England could be given cause for alarm.*

The Marqués de la Laguna agreed with his colleagues and added:

> *It would be against the Earl's own interest that he should go, for it is certain that as soon as he should arrive, or on the slightest pretext, he would be made the victim of some malicious plot . . . If he should still insist on going, Your Majesty should do nothing to force him to stay because of the extra expense and trouble this would involve.*

King Philip agreed with these recommendations of his Council, but it was not until 19 October that his answer to O Neill's memorial of 15 July was despatched to Rome. Far from committing himself in any way, the King merely instructed his ambassador to assure O Neill of his good will, to advise him to consider well the risk he would be taking and to use prudence and judgement in deciding what would suit him best. Meanwhile, the English agent in Brussels had renewed King James' offer to O Neill and, from Rome, Castro had written again to Madrid, pressing for a prompt reply, pointing out the urgency of the matter and enclosing a further memorial from the Earl. In this memorial, written in the third person after the manner of such documents, O Neill appeared to accept King Philip's unwillingness to give support to a military expedition to Ireland, yet it is clear that the possibility was still uppermost in his mind:

> God has been pleased to move the heart of the King of England who has offered the Earl peace, the restoration of his estates and admission to favour. The Earl would never accept this offer were it not for many reasons, the first and strongest of which is that he sees clearly he may no longer hope for aid for his cause from His Catholic Majesty unless a change of circumstances should force him to give this aid, which is very uncertain. Experience proves that such is the case for, if His Majesty had any intention of sending aid to the poor kingdom of Ireland or of ever removing it from the power of the heretics, now or never is the time, for the catholics of that kingdom have never been so united and so strongly in league for a rising against the heretics with any help, no matter how small, nor was there ever a time so opportune as the present to make war on an enemy who is now so lacking in money and troops; all the nobles of the kingdom of Scotland are on the point of rising against that enemy and await nothing more than to see the fires alight in Ireland, and all that is needed for this in Ireland is the presence of the Earl of Tiron. This being so, as in truth it is, and seeing that His Catholic Majesty, who has such a good opportunity of helping the catholics, does not bestir himself, is a sign that he is indifferent to their cause for the present.
>
> Therefore, the Earl of Tiron, considering the age which is upon him, the delay of help from Spain, the continuous danger to his life, not only because of his circumstances, but also because of the climate of this land where his sons and vassals who came with him have perished, considering also that were he to die before being restored to his estates, the King of England would never give possession of them to his surviving sons, nor to any of his house . . . the said Earl, although it may cost him his life, wishes to accept the reconciliation which the King of England may offer him . . . In order to achieve this, all he needs is His Catholic Majesty's permission to go to Flanders where he may carry out the negotiations and correspond more easily with his vassals as well as with the Council of England pending the settlement of his affairs.

King Philip's letter of 19 October 1613 appears to have taken an unaccountably long time to reach his ambassador in Rome, and it was only on 29 January 1614 that Castro acknowledged it and reported that he had made its contents known to O Neill. The Earl, he wrote, expressed his gratitude for the King's good will; he was aware of the danger to which he exposed himself by accepting the King of England's offer, but he had decided to do so; and, the ambassador continued:

> In order that his decision may have effect, the Earl begs Your Majesty to

give the necessary order for his removal to the States of Flanders where his sons are serving Your Majesty, and to give the order also that, in case the King of England's promises should turn out to be vain (as he suspects), he be allowed to remain in the said States of Flanders and receive there the financial aid which he has received here from Your Majesty until such a time as God may dispose otherwise.

O Neill asked also that three of his compatriots be allowed to go with him to Flanders. They are named in Castro's letter as Juan Daveto, or Seán Mac Daibhéid, and Eugenio Bardeo, or Eóghan Mac an Bhaird, the Tyrconnell poet, both of whom had left Ireland with the Earls, and Guillermo Miagh, or William Meade, who is described as a person of great courage who would be of great importance to the plans of the Earl. The ambassador added the following post script to his letter:

I see how much the Earl deserves and I cannot refrain from begging Your Majesty to be pleased to grant him all that for which he petitions, and to order that the decree for his travelling expenses be sent quickly, for any delay could cause him grave harm.

However, too much time had already been lost and King James no longer showed interest in O Neill's terms of reconciliation. From Brussels, on 11 February 1614, the Marqués de Guadaleste reported to King Philip:

The Secretary of the embassy of the King of England, who resides here, was making great efforts, through the intermediary of the Guardian of the Irish monastery of Louvain, to reduce the Earl of Tiron to the obedience of that King. These efforts have now ceased, since they have considered they could overcome the troubles which had broken out in that island of Ireland. And so, although the friar himself has spoken to him [the secretary], *he was answered that there was nothing more to say.*

King Philip was kept informed of developments in Ireland by his ambassador in London who reported on the stormy proceedings of the Dublin parliament of 1613-15 and on the difficulties which faced the catholic members of the opposition, some of whom made representations to King James and were imprisoned and fined on matters of religion. The Spanish ambassador in London was then Don Diego Sarmiento de Acuña, later created Conde de Gondomar. Unlike his two predecessors, who saw advantages to be gained by supporting O Neill in a military expedition to Ireland, Sarmiento favoured a policy of appeasement as a means of inducing King James to relax the severity of his laws against catholics, a view which had the full support of the Duke of Lerma and King Philip. Consequently O Neill was refused permission to go to Flanders and Philip wrote to Castro:

As it is my wish that the persecution of the Catholics in Ireland be not

intensified and that the King of England be not further incensed against them, it
would be well that you speak to the Pope on my behalf and tell him it would be
advisable that, for the present, he should not allow the Earl of Tiron to leave
Rome. Neither should His Holiness give ear to any new plans which may be
suggested to him over there.

But Pope Paul was not inclined to listen to any new plans of the Irish.
A few months earlier he had rejected their proposal for a re-conquest of
Ireland; he believed, his Secretary of State reported, such an enterprise was
not possible unless Spain declared war on England and, in that case, he
would not fail to provide what help he could, for the Irish catholics
deserved to be aided and favoured by the Holy See because of their
sufferings for the catholic religion and their constancy in the holy faith.
The Archbishop of Armagh, Peter Lombard, was an influential theologian
at the Vatican and was among those in favour of a conciliatory policy
towards King James. The Waterford-born Archbishop had supported O
Neill's war against Queen Elizabeth, but now he believed that Irish catholics would fare better and would not suffer for their religion if they
convinced King James of their loyalty to him.

These views cannot have been welcome to O Neill whose own
experience and personal acquaintance with King James and his ministers
had led him to other conclusions. King Philip's refusal to allow him go to
Flanders was another disappointment, but he did not lose hope and, since it
was important to keep Philip's good will, Castro wrote to the King on
behalf of O Neill:

Before I received Your Majesty's letters of the 15th of March the Earl of
Tiron had already decided to remain here until he saw what shape the affairs of
England would take. Nevertheless I made known to the Earl Your Majesty's
royal wishes and, apart from conforming with them as he will always do, he says
that even if he had secured a whole fleet for the conquest of his estates he would
leave it aside completely in order only to obey and give pleasure to Your
Majesty.

It is interesting to note that when O Neill suffered a refusal from King
Philip for any of his own plans, he usually took the opportunity, shortly
afterwards, of recommending one of his companions in exile for some
favour which the King felt obliged to grant. On this occasion, it was the
Countess of Tyrone who petitioned the King on behalf of her brother,
Edmund Magennis, and he was granted a monthly allowance of thirty
crowns.

While working towards his main objective of a return to Ireland on
his own terms, O Neill also sought means of consolidating his position and
that of his family abroad. In October 1612 he asked King Philip to be
sponsor to his son, Brian, on the occasion of the boy's confirmation, and to
nominate one of his ministers in Flanders to represent him at the cere-

mony.   Always fearful of offending the King of England, Philip ordered his ambassador in Brussels, the Marqués de Guadaleste, to act as sponsor, but not in the King's name.   This fine distinction made little difference for, as Guadaleste pointed out to the Irish Franciscan who was Brian's tutor, he was the King's representative anyway by virtue of his post as ambassador. The Archduke Albert had no such qualms and nominated Don Pedro de Toledo to act as sponsor in his name. Don Pedro was a grandee of Spain who held the titles of Marqués de Villafranca and Duque de Fernandina; he had been Philip's ambassador to the King of France, member of the Council of State, and was later Governor of Milan. On the 31 March 1613, Guadaleste wrote to the King concerning the boy's confirmation:

> *On Thursday 7th of this month the son of the Earl of Tiron was confirmed by the hand, and in the house of the Archbishop of Malines. His Highness, wishing to honour him, ordered Don Pedro de Toledo to act as godfather in his name, and I acted on behalf of Your Majesty. He was given the names of Philip and Albert. I gave the child a chain worth a hundred ducats and entertained him to a banquet, after which they returned to Louvain very pleased and grateful for the great favour shown by Your Majesty.*

After his confirmation, O Neill's young son was admitted as page at the court of the Archduke and he was called by his confirmation name of Philip, in honour of his royal godfather. His short life came to a tragic end in August 1617, when he was found strangled in his lodgings in Brussels. King Philip was informed of the boy's death by the secretary of his embassy in Flanders, Don Pedro Sarigo Ribera, who was chargé d'affaires since the death of Guadaleste in August of the previous year;   the secretary's letter is dated 7 September 1617:

> *On Wednesday the 16th of last month, when Don Phelippe Onel, second son of the Earl of Tiron returned from the school of the Jesuits to his house, he shut himself up in a room to which he was accustomed to retire. He is the boy to whom, by order of Your Majesty, the Marqués de Guadaleste was godfather in confirmation. When, after a long time, he had not come out, they went in to see what he was doing and they found him hanged. They do not know if he himself did it or if he was hanged by someone else, but it is feared that the latter is more likely because, apart from the fact that the boy was so well-disposed and was such a good christian, he was only eleven years old. They found him with his feet tied and a very slim hempen cord wound twice around his neck; the nail to which the cord was fastened was very short and blunt, and so it is suspected that he was strangled and was hanged afterwards in this manner in order to hide the fact. Two of his servants are under arrest and an enquiry is under way but, up to the present, nothing of importance has been found.*

Brian O Neill was buried in the Franciscan monastery at Louvain. No stone marks his grave.

In 1613, Brian's older brother, John, had also been received at the court of Flanders as page to the Infanta Isabel. He was titular colonel of the Irish regiment but, being only fourteen years of age, he was still pursuing his studies and did not begin his military career until 1615. In September 1614, with a view to the advancement of his son, the Earl of Tyrone asked King Philip to grant him a knighthood of one of the three military orders of Spain. The Conde de Castro transmitted O Neill's request to the King and noted that it was customary to grant such an honour to the sons of principal noblemen who had finished their service as pages.   Founded in the 12th century, the Spanish military orders of chivalry of Santiago, Calatrava and Alcántara carried enormous prestige; moreover, a knight commander received the income of an estate, or commandery, of his order. By 1614 when O Neill requested the honour for his son, three other Irish boys had already been admitted as knights of the order of Santiago; they were the two sons of O Sullivan Beare and the son of MacWilliam Burke, all three of whom served as pages at the court of Philip III.   In November 1614, the Infanta Isabel wrote in strong support of O Neill's request and the King agreed   but, whatever the reason, nothing more was done and it was not until 1632 that John O Neill was made knight commander of the order of Calatrava.

In 1615, John's father planned for him a marriage alliance with a family of influence and wealth, and in July of that year Father Robert Chamberlain arrived in Brussels sent by the Earl to arrange a marriage between John and the daughter of Don Juan de Mancicidor, the Archduke's secretary of state for war.   It was not long before the English ambassador, Sir William Trumbull,   found out the purpose of Father Chamberlain's visit to Brussels and he wrote to the Secretary of State in London, Sir Ralph Winwood:

> Righ honourable, having an eye still upon the alliance in treaty between the Irish colonel and the daughter of Secretary Mancisador, which now seemeth to grow more mature than when I formerly wrote thereof to your honour, it was my chance to light upon a letter . . . by the assistance of the party which gave me notice of that business; so that now . . . I am verily persuaded of the truth of that information, and think it is high time some underhand means were used to prevent the match.

Shortly afterwards, the ambassador was able to report that 'a good patriot' had put forward, as arguments against the marriage, that the Earl of Tyrone was a 'usurper' and had never been a sovereign prince, that he was a vassal to the crown of England and, having been attainted of high treason, all his lands had been confiscated and he had no other revenue than his monthly pension, and that, if such a marriage took place, the English government would be provoked into expelling all the remaining Roman catholics from Ulster and planting heretics in their place, and, the ambassador concludes:

With these allegations, it is hoped that malevolent conjunction will be broken, and the colonel left to seek a wife elsewhere.

In view of the policy of conciliation which was then pursued by the Papacy and by the Spanish government, the final point of the argument could not have been better chosen and the marriage was effectively prevented.

CHAPTER SEVEN

'Destruction by Peace'

In October 1614 the packed and coerced Irish parliament passed a bill for the attainder of O Neill, O Donnell and their followers and for the confiscation of their lands, which amounted to over two million acres. News of this event reached Rome within a few weeks but, far from being disheartened, the Irish exiles were roused to furious activity. Despite O Neill's age, and the reverses, betrayals and endless misfortunes he had suffered for over twelve years, he now set about organising his most vigorous attempt to return to Ireland with military support. On this occasion he stirred up so many people of influence in Spain, Italy and Flanders that it seemed this attempt was bound to succeed.

Excitement grew in Ireland as messengers arrived from Rome with instructions from O Neill and news of his impending return. There was alarm in England as spies sent in their reports from Italy, Spain and Flanders. All Irish persons returning from these countries were treated as suspect and closely questioned by order of Chichester.

It was rumoured that O Neill was about to leave Rome for Flanders or for Spain. From Brussels the English ambassador reported that O Neill had given orders to have 'some of his countrymen employed at sea in ships-of-war, as pirates, with commission to take all vessels that come in their way, until they be increased to the number of twenty sail, or thereabouts, and then to make their descent on some convenient part of Ireland, not only to find malcontents enough of that realm to join with them, but to be assisted with forces from the King of Spain.'

English ambassadors in France and Flanders were instructed to protest against the supposed admission of O Neill into those countries. All movements of the Irish regiment in Flanders were carefully reported to London by English agents, for King James was far from confident that Philip would not give support to an Irish insurrection.

In London the Spanish ambassador was visited by the English Secretary of State who told him that King James was very disturbed at the reported news of O Neill's move to Flanders, that he objected strongly to King Philip's support of these rebels, and asked that they not be allowed into Flanders. So strongly, indeed, did the Secretary express himself that the ambassador concluded his report to Madrid on this interview by adding:

And what I myself believe is that, if the Earl [of Tyrone] had remained here, either they would have cut off his head, or else he would now be in prison for no other sin than having refused to be a sinner.

While the English ambassador in Brussels was endeavouring to obtain from the Archduke a promise that he prevent O Neill from entering Flanders, in Rome O Neill was busy laying plans that had nothing to do with a journey to those states. On 23 May 1615 he wrote to Archbishop Conry in Madrid enclosing letters for the Duke of Lerma and several other ministers. On the same day he wrote also to Andrés Velázquez, member of the Council of State with special responsibility for the secret service. In his lengthy but remarkably well ordered letter to Velázquez, O Neill outlines the situation in Ireland, points to the urgency of military aid, and declares:

We are resolved, those of us alive today, that we shall not wait to see the shameful day when the English completely conquer our provinces, profane our temples and seduce our children to their service. With our lives we shall procure the remedy for now, with the knife at our throats, to delay would be the surest misfortune.

With all the eloquence at his command, O Neill then puts forward the advantages which he believes Spain would derive from the projected invasion, were its success ensured by the minimum of help from Spain, and adds:

In matters of state it is clear that an inevitable enemy such as the kingdom of England becomes more powerful in the shelter of its peace treaties than through its own strength, and if the peace with Spain did not exist and England's strength were put to the test, I should be in no doubt as to the result, nor do I believe this result would be disastrous.

In the matter of His Majesty's prestige, the cause of Ireland is even more directly important. In the name of His Majesty and under his flags we have consumed our lives and our strength. We have held steadfastly to the hopes which he gave us. Today, on the point of total destruction, we throw ourselves at his feet as King and lord, not of our country, for despite our ardent endeavours it has not yet been our fortune that this should come to pass, but of our hearts and of our wishes, as we have proved by our actions. And what better cause, Señor, to break with England, if the cause of God be foremost, as it should be, in the eyes of Kings.

There are countless motives for, and abundant benefits to be derived from not being such extreme friends of the English who are of a different religion, whose plans are contrary to those of Spain and who declared their friendship for Spain merely for their own purposes and as a cloak for their deceits. And for this friend the King our lord will allow that Ireland be lost and with it the most devoted of his vassals, Ireland which he does not enter as King by conquest but acclaimed and loved by the people, where he does not come to inflict tyranny but to remove it, where the obligations we shall have to him must urge us to greater endeavours than the Spaniards themselves, where we shall become as a frontier to the English and to all the North.

We beg His Majesty to be moved to help us, remembering what the English have done many times despite their peace treaties with Spain: since the first rebellions of Flanders until today they have fomented these rebellions against His Majesty and continue to do so. They have given to these rebels of Spain the power they now hold. The English themselves, using the name of peace as a deception, teach us this manner of feigned friendship and of destruction by peace. We have seen this by experience in the treaties with France, the treaties with England, the truces with the States of Holland, the confederations and alliances with the Potentates of Germany, Italy and the Republics, for although all of them many times have helped, to the limit of their powers, the enemies of His Majesty, this has not been the cause of an open break for it has always been considered a lesser evil to combat the few who are being helped than to break with all. For the same reason when the war in Ireland will cause difficulty for him, the King of England will not break with Spain, even if he suspects that Spain is helping Ireland, for it will not be a good time to provoke open hostility with a powerful enemy.

The last and perhaps the strongest reason which could move His Majesty to help us is the consideration of which would be the greater evil: that we be lost, as we must be if he does not help us, leaving England victorious, free of all weakness in her monarchy and most powerful, or that, with moderate help, we maintain the catholic religion in the kingdom of Ireland, thereby causing such difficulties to the English that they may neither help the Dutch nor put into execution the plans they have made for their naval expeditions, and this they will certainly do as soon as they have the power.

I am sending you separately an account of the help which His Majesty could give us without weakening his forces or his resources and without giving the King of England apparent reason for complaint or cause for breaking the peace. May God grant it success since, for the sake of His Holy Faith and of our obligations we, catholics of Ireland, are offering our lives and His Majesty is our only hope . . .

I have sent to the Archbishop of Tuam letters for some of His Majesty's Ministers to inform them of my decision. If you think this would be of advantage, the letters could be given to them; otherwise let them be destroyed, for their contents are merely intended to inform them more fully of the case and in each letter I refer them to this account which I send you. May God keep you as I wish. Rome, 23 May 1615.

TIRON.

A brief account of the help required for the expedition was enclosed with O Neill's letter to Velázquez:

We ask that all the Irish catholics in His Majesty's kingdoms, particularly in the States of Flanders, from the Earl of Tiron down to the last soldier, return to their country. There they will fortify the catholic parts of the kingdom as they have done in the last wars, for they are experienced in such matters and have now gained much knowledge in Flanders and in Spain. This is of great importance for there is not one noble family in all Ireland which has not a son, a brother, or a cousin in His Majesty's service. If it should please His Majesty to grant us this favour, various means of bringing these men to Ireland without conspicuousness or inconvenience will be represented to His Majesty.

It will be necessary for His Majesty to help with munitions and arms for, since the peace, the English have taken great care to disarm the kingdom of Ireland by removing munitions and military equipment. If His Majesty is pleased to agree, the manner of providing these will be represented to him. The quantity will be so small as to be within possible limits and so that His Majesty be pleased to continue sending this help if we meet with initial success. The manner of sending the first amount with due secrecy will also be represented.

A certain amount of money will be necessary to send some persons to Ireland for secret negotiations and to provide food and gunpowder for the castles of the cities which are to be captured at the first uprising so as to enable them to withstand a siege and await reinforcement. The smallest amount with which this may be done is fifty thousand ducats.

The greatest help which could be given to us would be that four or six experienced and trustworthy persons be ordered by His Majesty to come with us. They would bear witness to the good will with which we commit ourselves to this undertaking, and, to them, we would hand over, in the name of His Majesty, the castles and fortresses we capture.

When these letters from O Neill arrived in Madrid at the end of June, King Philip and his court were in Valladolid. Archbishop Conry and O Neill's other representatives had several consultations with Velázquez in Madrid, as a result of which the Councillor took it upon himself to present their case to the Duke of Lerma in Valladolid. He forwarded to him the documents he had received from O Neill together with a carefully worded explanatory letter from himself:

The Archbishop of Tuam wished to see Your Excellency to give an account of the Earl of Tiron's decision and to bring you the enclosed letter from him. The Earl has also sent letters to the Archbishop and to me, giving me authority to act in the matter according to my judgement. Using this authority, I have advised the Archbishop against making the journey to visit you for the Ambassador of England watches his movements and those of all the Irish here. The Earl's letter to me and the other papers he sends will show Your Excellency what his plan is and that he is driven to it by the necessity which leaves him no other choice of action.

I do not doubt that the machinations of the King of England and all the other circumstances described by the Earl are as he states them to be, for I already had knowledge of these from English and Irish people and have informed Your Excellency accordingly.

I have had several conversations with the Archbishop, with Don Juan Batheo, Don Guillermo Miagh and the Lord of Biraven and I have endeavoured to find if there were, in the Earl's decision, any personal ulterior motive. Although I have seen each of these Irishmen separately and repeatedly and have brought the conversation to these matters, I have always found them to agree in saying that their countrymen are calling them and assuring them that if help is not sent to them they will perish miserably at the hands of their enemies, that they are ready to avenge themselves and to die for their country, that once the rising has started, aid from Spain will be necessary for its success and that any delay now would be fatal. They have told me that the lives of their fathers, their sons and their brothers are at stake and for this reason they have taken their decision regardless of the risks involved.

Since the arrival from Rome of the last ordinary which left that city on the 3rd of last month and arrived here on the 22nd they have been pressing me with these arguments. I have restrained them saying that I am awaiting news from England and telling them to be of good heart. They assure me that their information is correct and that they had no choice in making their decision. They say that, even if their fears were unfounded, age is coming upon the Earl and the other catholic leaders in whom their hopes are centred and, when these leaders are dead, the English will have little trouble in overcoming the rest.

In the meantime I have wished to give Your Excellency an account of all this and to submit to you the papers which are here enclosed so that when His Majesty has seen them a suitable answer may be decided upon. The delay I have imposed on the Irish leaves the door open for any answer whether it be giving them hope or denying it. If it is judged advisable that help be given to them as coming from a prelate moved by devotion to the catholic cause, this could be done through the Archbishop of Toledo. Fifty thousand ducats would be sufficient for their purpose and this amount would not seem much as coming from His Grace, nor would it be so large as to appear to come from His Majesty. His Majesty and Your Excellency will take the decision.

The cause is worthy and I see the Irish determined in their purpose, for already from Rome they have sent several persons to raise the people through the intermediary of the priests of their nation. In three cities they have enlisted eight thousand men who are ready to join with them in one day or even one hour. In the mountains they have others ready to take the passes and they say that they intend to gain that kingdom for His Majesty in a single day or to die defending it.

I understand also that, although they have such great esteem for the Earl of Tiron, they would not make him their king for there are other catholics who only recognise him as their leader because of his personal talents and the fortunes of war and obey him willingly in wartime but would not recognise him as their lord.

This is a matter of great consequence and worty of consideration for, although it must create a diversion for the enemies of His Majesty, it must also stir up trouble. If the Irish are to be helped openly, much thought must be given to the uniting of so much of His Majesty's forces at sea. If not, although they are ready to start this undertaking on their own, it would seem necessary to throw in at least a few ships and to reinforce these with the corsairs who are a wonderful cover because of the number of insubordinate and unruly men among them. In this manner the help given would not be apparent and it would be easy to have tidings brought to us and information sent back. Also, if this is to be done on a larger scale, ships from the Atlantic fleet and from the ports of Guipuzcoa and Vizcaya could be used to form a good force at sea.

I think the Earl of Tiron will leave Rome shortly for Genoa where, in disguise, he will await His Majesty's answer and embark on a ship which some Irish merchant friends of his will hold in readiness. They want to be in Ireland for the feast of St. Michael for that is the day on which new English magistrates are appointed in all the cities and towns of that kingdom. At that time they will rise, take up arms and put their plan into execution. May God enlighten and guide them and may He keep Your Excellency for the direction of such important matters. Madrid, 4 July 1615.

Andrés Velazquez.

Velázquez had good reason to suggest that fifty thousand ducats 'would not seem much as coming from His Grace' of Toledo, for the Archbishop was an uncle of the Duke of Lerma and was one of many relatives of the Duke's who were enriched through the favourite's limitless influence over the King.

On 12 July, having received no answer to his letters of 23 May, O Neill wrote again pressingly to Velázquez: '. . . By the entrails of Christ I beg you to have an answer sent to me that I may decide on my course of action.'

It was not until 31 July that the Spanish Council of State in Valladolid discussed O Neill's letters. The members of the Council were careful to express no opinion that might not be in keeping with the policy of the powerful Duke of Lerma. The unanimous recommendation of the six members present was not only that no help of any description be given to the Irish but also that O Neill be warned that, if he left Rome without express order from King Philip, his allowance would be stopped. The reasons given amounted to the following: It is not the time to have trouble with England when the present aim is to maintain peace with the English King who is anxious to have good relations with Spain. The Royal Treasury is not sufficient for new undertakings, not even for those which are necessary. There is no naval power to compete with that of England and Holland; therefore any effort made in that direction would be wasted and the expenses lost.

Finally, Velázquez was rebuked for meddling in matters which required extreme circumspection and, it was stated, although, as was right, he had authority to deal with minor matters he should be reminded not to deal with those of greater importance without express order.

King Philip's approval and support for the reconquest of Ireland was an essential part of O Neill's plan. For the immediate purpose of casting off the rule of protestant England, O Neill believed that Irish and old English catholics would now unite under his leadership, but such unity would only last as long as the war. Once the reconquest was effected, it would be necessary to substitute the authority of King Philip to that of King James, and to establish a government in which the various interests of the country would be represented under the presidency of a Spanish Viceroy. Consequently Philip's agreement for the expedition was of the utmost importance. The refusal of Spain to subscribe to his plan was a bitter blow to O Neill and his supporters. The feast of St Michael in 1615, which was to be their day of victory, brought only the reminder of another opportunity lost 'through lack of help from a Christian Prince' and it was little consolation that, in the words of O Neill, the Irish could well 'call God and his Saints to witness that it was not because their courage had failed them.'

In Madrid, Archbishop Conry continued to argue in favour of sending help to Ireland. Early in September he wrote to Velázquez:

Despite all the arguments put forward in writing by the Earl of Tiron as regards our afflicted country and despite what I said to you concerning the present urgent necessity which suffers no delay, within the last few days you have answered me that now is not the time and that the Earl should remain quietly in Rome. I have written to him in those terms in order to comply with my obligation, but I fear that he is resolved to risk his life, since he can do no more, before the English forestall all possible moves and complete the ruin of what little remains in the country. So that you may realise the urgency of the situation, the irretrievable loss any delay would cause, and with what little help more could be achieved now than ever before, I send you the following information which I have just received from a very sure source . . .

First, the King of England . . . has ordered that the eldest sons of all the principal gentlemen of the kingdom be sent to England in order to hold their fathers in subjection and to prevent any rising within the kingdom, and in order to bring them up in their sect and to impoverish their fathers by this continuous expense for their sons.

2. He asks the parliament for an intolerable subsidy to the value of the fourth part of their income and the third part of their personal property.

3. He holds prisoner at present in the Castle of Dublin six of the principal gentlemen of the province of Ulster, one of whom is a nephew of the Earl of Tiron, and the others are his close rleatives. They are accused of wishing to take possession of all the strongholds of that province; letters have been received from over there which say that, whether this be true or not, they will be beheaded and that the others will eventually suffer the same fate.

    4. The Earl of Tomond, president and captain-general of the province of Munster, is at present visiting the cities of that province, accompanied by certain English officials, and they are taking rigorous measures. It is believed that they fear some movement from the catholics, which they wish to forestall.

    5. It is known as a certainty that the lord of Ile and Quyntile in Scotland has escaped from the Castle of Edenburgo in Scotland. He is an uncle of the Earl of Tirconell who is in Flanders and is one of the most powerful lords of the kingdom of Scotland . . . and now he is in arms with one thousand five hundred soldiers in his territory of the Isles. His lands are at a distance of only three hours' navigation from those of the Earls, to whom the occasion of this revolt would have been of the greatest importance if the Earl of Tiron had been there for, with very little help, this gentleman could move all Scotland to revolt and they would be of great help to one another in view of their vicinity, their kinship and the strength of their territories . . . I beg you to represent these matters to His Majesty.

Velázquez wrote to the Duke of Lerma, enclosing the Archbishop's letter and explaining further:

    The Archbishop and the other Irish are very insistent that His Majesty should be asked to allow the Irish regiment in Flanders and the Earl of Tiron to go to Ireland. With this help alone they would undertake to reduce that kingdom to the obedience of the Roman Church and of His Majesty. The Earl of Tiron has also written to the Archbishop that he wishes to come in secret to pay his respects to His Majesty and Your Excellency, to represent the miserable state of his country and to receive here the last blessing for the resolution he is forced to take by the design of the King of England.

But it was not to be expected that Lerma and the King would reverse their decision. Nevertheless O Neill persisted in his efforts. In October 1615, when news reached Rome that James MacDonnell, lord of Islay and Cantyre and kinsman of the Earl of Tyrconnell, had escaped from prison in Edinburgh and was leading a revolt in Scotland. O Neill asked the Spanish ambassador to inform King Philip 'in case it should be decided to help this gentleman in some way against the English.' Once again, the answer was: 'In view of the peace with England, it is not the time to consider such matters.'

At this time, more bitter to O Neill than Philip's persistent refusal, was the news of his son Conn. Until the early summer of 1615 Conn was held at Charlemont Fort in the custody of an English captain, Sir Tobias Caulfield. Following the discovery of a plot to release the fourteen-year-old boy and get him to Flanders, he was taken to Dublin and, on the order of King James, he was sent into England. It was concerning this boy that, a few weeks earlier, O Neill had written in anger: 'A son of mine is even now being reared in heresy, but I trust in God that the blood he has in his veins will not permit such a deception and that one day he will avenge for me this outrage.'

The plot for Conn's release was part of a larger conspiracy in which many young Ulster men were involved. They had intended to capture Derry, Coleraine and other northern strongholds and to obtain the freedom of their kinsmen imprisoned in the Tower of London. They were betrayed. Twenty-five of the conspirators were arrested and, at Derry on 31st July 1615, six of them were condemned to be hanged, drawn and quartered. Among these was O Neill's nephew, Brian Crosach, son of Cormac O Neill.

It is not difficult to imagine what must have been the feelings of the Earl of Tyrone. A few short years had seen the death of two sons and of countless close relatives, friends and supporters, many of them executed by his enemies. He was convinced that, in view of England's weak position, the reconquest of Ireland could be achieved with very little help from Spain, yet all his attempts to force an agreement from Philip had failed, and it was not even possible for him to approach the King in person. He was forced to remain in Rome, but he continued to watch for a favourable turn of events and to petition the King in favour of his companions in exile.

In November 1615, Castro wrote on O Neill's behalf in recommendation of John Rath, the captain of the ship in which the Earls had sailed from Lough Swilly. In December, he asked that an allowance be granted to his nephew, John O Neill, brother of Brian Crosach who had been executed in Ireland. Shortly afterwards, expressing concern at the efforts of English agents to destroy the Irish regiment in Flanders, he asked that suitable measures be taken to ensure its preservation.

O Neill was now sixty-five years of age but there is no indication that his health was failing, nor indeed that his spirit was broken. On the contrary, he grasped every opportunity with buoyant courage and appeared to bear his trials with remarkable fortitude. In September 1615, an English spy who had spent some time in Rome sent a report to London with some details of O Neill's circumstances at that time. He was one Thomas Doyne, alias George White, a medical doctor, and he wrote from Venice:

> *Now I have more at large to write unto you, for I was as near to Tyrone and his wife, for the space of two months daily as any that was in the palace. It was my fortune that she was sick at my coming into the town, and Doctor Barnardin, which is their doctor, could do her no good; but as soon as she heard of me coming into the palace, she sent for me and told me of her disease. With what I did for her she began to be better and better. When Tyrone saw it he was very familiar with me and had me lodge in his palace. He goes often to the Spanish ambassador's house. He is well beloved from the Pope, and from all those which are under him, and especially he that thinks to be Pope after the death of this man. Last Easter he sent Tyrone a present, and desired him to be of a good*

courage, and that God keepeth him for to have some comfort in his country hereafter. Though a man would think he is an old man by sight: no, he is lusty and strong, and well able to travel; for a month ago, at evening, when his frere and his gentlemen were all with him, they were talking of England and Ireland, and he drew out his sword: 'His Majesty', said he, 'thinks that I am not strong. I would he that hates me most in England were with me to see whether I am strong or no.' These that were by said: 'We would we were with forty thousand pounds of money in Ireland, to see what we should do.' Whereon Tyrone remarked: 'If I be not in Ireland within these two years, I will never desire more to look for it.' This is the discourse Tyrone and his companions had.

Posts every Thursday with letters from Spain, from Flanders every Friday. Many pensioners go to Ireland, but for no goodness, for if the King of Spain can do anything there, they will take his part before any other . . . Tyrone's wife is young and fair . . . . Her foster sister is gone for Ireland; her husband came out of Ireland against [to] her and brought all the news and secrets that he could unto Tyrone and brought with him such secrets as Tyrone could afford him withal. His name is Nicholas Hollawood, dwelling three miles of Dublin his city.

There is another politic fellow, called Shean Crone Mc Dived; he went to the city of Burdeus [Bordeaux], and parted from thence into Spain, and wrote unto Tyrone all the news he had from Ireland. The Archbishop in Spain,   and the freres in Flanders,   receive letters every three months from Ireland. There is but few things done in the court of Ireland, let it be ever so secret, but it will be heard, or else sought out by them; for the Jesuits and freres of Ireland have such good friends about the court which brings them news, wherein that your honour may be assured of. As I am a true servant unto your honour, if you do not take some other course, for all your policy and wisdoms, you will be deceived. Tyrone sent for his son in Ireland. Those that promised and that would perform it if they could do it, shall be very well considered for their pains, but there came news unto them that he was brought into England some two months past, the which news grieved them. Thus I end, at Venice, the 17th of September 1615.

Your humble servant,

Thomas Doyne.

P.S. Sixteen ounces of blood I took out of Tyrone's legs drawn by boxinge glasses, the which for the space of thirteen days he would have me come unto him, unto his bedstead, afore he will get out of his bed, to confer and talk with him, and to see how he did.

Bleeding a patient by boxing, or cupping-glasses, or by leeches, was then a very common remedy, even for minor illnesses, and Doyne's letter does not suggest that the Earl was suffering from any serious illness at that time.

On 7 January 1616, O Neill signed a glowing testimonial for Pedro Blanco, a Spanish survivor of the Armada of 1588, whom he had received and befriended.   After the wreck of his ship, the *Juliana*,   off the coast of Sligo, Pedro Blanco and several of his companions were guided to the safety of O Neill's territory and remained there for many years. Pedro, the last survivor of this group, accompanied the Earls to Flanders and to Rome and, in his testimonial, O Neill praised his loyalty and his courage during the war years and, referring to the battle of the Yellow Ford, he wrote:

> *He also distinguished himself in another battle at which I was present and where we slew the general and the greater part of his army; there, I myself saw Pedro Blanco fighting so valiantly that I never afterwards wanted to be parted from him.*

It is worthy of note that O Neill signed this document with his own hand. If, as was claimed by his enemies, he became blind, it cannot have been before January 1616. There are no references to his alleged blindness in Spanish records, and it should be noted also that, as early as 1610, Chichester was attempting to spread the rumour that the Earl had become blind in order to discourage his supporters in Ireland and reduce them to obedience.

On the 9 January 1616, Castro wrote to King Philip on behalf of O Neill:

> *Seeing how adverse the climate of this country is to the health of the Countess, his wife, the Earl of Tiron has resolved to give her permission to go to live in Flanders, and because this permission cannot have effect without the protection and help of Your Majesty, for the Earl has no money with which to meet the expenses of such a long journey, he has asked me to represent this to Your Majesty and to beg you, as I do, to order that he be granted the necessary amount so that his wife may travel in all comfort, with a sufficient escort and in a manner suited to her quality. It seems to me that this is a very reasonable request.*

It is possible that O Neill was worried about his wife's health, but it is more likely that this was an attempt to send some trusted friends of his to Flanders to further his plans. His request was refused and King Philip wrote to the ambassador: 'As regards the Countess of Tiron's journey to Flanders, you will give to understand to the Earl, her husband, that it will be better for her to go to Naples or to Sicily.'

The fact that, after 9 January 1616, no further requests from O Neill were transmitted by the ambassador, would suggest that, shortly after that date, he became seriously ill. In Spanish records, I have found no references to his last illness, but this may be due to the fact that, early in 1616, Castro was recalled from Rome and was sent to Sicily as Viceroy. The man appointed to replace Castro in Rome was Cardinal Gaspar de Borja y Velasco, yet another descendant of St Francis Borgia and kinsman of the Duke of Lerma. One of his first letters to King Philip was to announce the death of O Neill which occurred on 20 July 1616:

The Earl of Tiron died on the 20th of this month in the same christian and exemplary manner in which he lived, leaving the Countess and those of his nation in great affliction and without the protection he afforded them. The Countess hopefully trusts Your Majesty will order that she be granted the Earl's allowance, for her house continues to be a refuge for the same people as before on whom her husband spent more than in ostentation or on his own comfort.

The Cardinal was of the opinion that this should be done and had already taken the decision of continuing the allowance to the Countess pending the King's decision. He reported also that he had paid for the expenses of the funeral, but, he added, in doing so he had been very careful and had 'endeavoured to cover appearances which could hinder the relations of Your Majesty with the King of England.

Cardinal Borja's letter was discussed at a meeting of the Spanish Council of State on 27 August 1616. The members of the Council were unanimous in approving the Cardinal's decision with regard to the expenses of O Neill's funeral. As for the allowance to the Countess, all but one were of the opinion that half the amount which O Neill received should be sufficient for his widow. This one dissenting member, whose advice was taken by Lerma and the King, was in favour of granting the full allowance because, he said:

The Countess is burdened with many dependents of the Earl who will continue to seek in her house the shelter and help to which they were accustomed. If they do not receive it there they will come here to agitate for and obtain greater favours for they have no other recourse or protection.

In his letter, Cardinal Borja assured King Philip that, while paying for the expenses of O Neill's funeral, he had 'endeavoured to cover appearances.' It would seem that the Cardinal had underestimated the efficiency of the English spy system for, on 17 August, Trumbull was able to write from Brussels to the Earl of Somerset:

I may now safely and truly by these confirm the news I wrote unto your honour by my last letters concerning the late Earl of Tyrone who died at Rome the 20th of July of a fever and was there buried with great pomp and solemnity at the charges of the Spanish ambassador.

Two days later, on 19 August, the English ambassador in Madrid, Sir Francis Cottington, reported to London:

The Earl of Tyrone is dead at Rome, by whose death this King saves five hundred ducats every month, for so much pension he had from here well paid him. Upon the news of his death, I observe that all the principal Irish entertained in several parts of this kingdom are repaired unto this court, as O Sullivan Bear, or Master of Bearhaven, from the Groyne [i.e. la Coruña]; Raymond Burke, from Lisbon; one who calls himself Desmond from

Bayonne [i.e. Bayona] *in Galicia; and the Archbishop of Tuam, from Alcalá, with many others of less note, but captains and of good quality.*

O Neill was buried in the church of San Pietro in Montorio, beside his son, the Baron of Dungannon, and his brothers-in-law, Ruairí and Cathbharr O Donnell. The brief inscription on his tombstone was still visible in 1832 and was recorded by Father C. P. Meehan:

D.O.M.
HIC. QUIESCUNT.
UGONIS. PRINCIPIS. O NEILL.
OSSA.

Since then it has disappeared, and the probability is that the flag-stone was reversed when the pavement of the church was repaired in 1848. The tombstones bearing the more lengthy and conspicuous epitaphs of the O Donnells and of the Baron of Dungannon were carefully replaced in position and are still to be seen.

O Neill died without achieving the aims which he had set himself, to repossess his ancestral lands, and:

to leave the kingdom of Ireland united to his [King Philip's] *monarchy and free from the yoke of English tyranny.*

He wished Ireland to be free to continue its own normal process of development under the protection of Spain. The nine years of his enforced exile were spent in persistent and unremitting effort towards those aims. Spanish sources provide clear evidence of this, and also of the fact that the so-called 'Flight of the Earls' was not a journey into voluntary exile, but a planned, tactical retreat and an attempt by O Neill to secure military aid by presenting his case in person to King Philip.

Appendix: Memorials of O Neill and O Donnell

Memorial of O Neill and O Donnell, undated but forwarded to King Philip III by the Conde de Fuentes with his letter of 13 April 1608.

Substance of the articles which the Earls of Tiron and Tirconel have written to His Catholic Majesty.

First, they have represented the services they rendered to the Church of God and to the Crown of Spain at the persuasion of King Philip II, may he be in glory, father of His Majesty. At his royal persuasion they waged war for the space of eleven years with the success which was known throughout Europe, gaining many signal victories in the course of which the enemies lost much infantry and artillery, and the flower of the nobility and militia of England perished; among those who were killed were seven generals and the Viceroy of Ireland, called the Baron Bures [i.e. Lord Burgh], about two hundred captains with many other soldiers and innumerable gentlemen and officers. As a result, and because of the taxes which Queen Elizabeth imposed on the English in order to maintain an army of sixteen to twenty thousand soldiers every year in that war of Ireland, they were forced to recall their experienced soldiers who were serving against Spain in Brittany in order to send them to Ireland; they were forced to stop sending their fleets to the coasts of the Indies and of Spain, excepting that which the Earl of Essex brought to Cádiz and this happened when the Queen had made a truce of four months with the Earls; they were forced to stop sending substantial help to the rebels of Holland during all the time of the said war; they were finally brought to such straits that they were forced to coin money of copper instead of silver and they were on the point of losing both England and Ireland if the Earls had received help at the right time. Moreover, when the said Queen died, the English were so exhausted from the war in Ireland and so hopeless of being able to maintain themselves with their strength alone that they surrendered to the Scot and chose him for their King, despite the fact that those two nations are great enemies.

Although, against the heretics of England, God was pleased to use the said Earls as sole instruments for these great deeds in his service and in that of the Crown of Spain, nevertheless, for His hidden purposes, He allowed that they should lack all human help and that almost all of them be lost for, when already the greater part of their sons, brothers, kinsfolk and principal persons were lost in that war, and when they had spent their wealth and that of their vassals, it happened then that the help which His Majesty sent, and for which they had waited so long, came to land in the province of Munster which is far removed from them. In mid-winter they had to march a distance of about one hundred leagues through enemy territory, passing many rivers and forced to make many bridges; finally they suffered a misfortune on the day that they went to the aid of Don Juan del Aguila who was besieged in Quinsal. This obliged them to return to their lands and to send to Spain one from among their number, the Conde Odonel, to beg Your Majesty to send them some help to save their lives; and although they were then hard pressed, they continued the war for two years more, persevering firmly in the league and hoping that the said Conde Odonel would bring them help, until his death was announced. Then the English and the Irish lords who were with them closed in on them with many armies, planting so many garrisons in their lands that they were prevented from sowing and cultivating the land. The Catholics came to suffer such extreme want that they were forced to eat human flesh and, of the vassals of the said Earls, more than sixty thousand died of sheer hunger, which obliged the Earls to surrender to their enemies, for they found themselves bereft of all human assistance.

Thus, in order to serve Your Majesty, the Earls have lost many lives, estates and possessions, for at the time of the truce, at the beginning of the war when they were offered honourable conditions of peace, they renewed the war solely because of the letters which Alonso Cobos brought to them from His Majesty Philip II, may he be in glory, and they continued the war because from time to time they received similar letters from His Majesty, until, as has been said, they were forced to surrender to their enemies.

But this did not discourage the Earls from the service of His Majesty, for they sent a titled lord of their lands, named Maculliam Burc, and several other persons who came in His Majesty's service in secret from time to time, and in particular they sent a message to the Conde de Villamediana when he was ambassador of Spain in England, offering to be of service to His Majesty if peace with England did not come to be established, and to lead a rising in the Kingdom of Ireland. This is the extent of the services and of the losses of the Earls.

When the Earls had finally concluded an agreement with the English Queen, she died; this King, who was King of Scotland, became King of England, and he took as ministers the same men who had been the Queen's Councillors. On account of the last war these ministers nourished feelings of hatred towards the Earls and persecuted and tyrannised them for the space of three or four years, forcing their vassals to deny the holy faith, executing many of them, and every day depriving the Earls of some of their estates. In matters of religion they tyrannised and persecuted all the gentlemen and nobles of the Kingdom, as well as the common people, for they suspected that they might join the Earls in waging war once again. When the principal nobles of Ireland saw the fury of the persecution and of the tyranny, and as they were rendered desperate by the prospect of a succession of heretics inheriting the Crown of England, they had secret meetings with the Earls and swore to them that whenever they would take up arms they would assist them unto death and they begged the Earls to send for help to the King of Spain for they would give him the whole kingdom. When the English saw the Irish so united and the great respect and devotion shown to the Earls, and when they considered what the Earls had previously accomplished and what they might do again, the King of England, although he knew nothing of their secret dealings, summoned them to England on the suggestion of his ministers. The Earls were advised by intimate friends of theirs on the King's very Council that their only choices were to die, to take up arms, or to escape; so as not to disturb the kingdom and the peace without orders from His Catholic Majesty, they chose to leave all their estates and their vassals and to escape with their lives and, having made that decision, they hurried to a sea port of their country and, leaving their horses on the shore with no one to hold their bridles, they went aboard a ship to the number of about one hundred persons, including soldiers, women and principal gentlemen, among whom was the lord Maguire, cousin of the said Earls, who left an estate of sixty uninterrupted miles. They intended to disembark in Spain, but contrary winds forced them to land at a port of Normandy in France where they were held until the King of France ordered them to be freed and gave them permission to go to Flanders, but he did not wish to give them permission to go to Spain.

Their Highnesses received them with great affection and honour and, as they set out on their journey to Spain, they received an order from His Majesty desiring them to suspend their voyage to Spain, to send him in writing an account of their claims and intentions and to await his reply. The Archduke pressed them to leave his States in order to satisfy the English and to fulfill a promise he had made to the English ambassador at the beginning when he thought that the Earls were going to Spain and that His Majesty had given no other orders. They complied with his wishes and, leaving behind them in Flanders those of their people whom they could not bring, they went to Milan bringing with them those whose presence was most necessary and trusting in the honour and noble feelings of His Excellency the Conde de Fuentes to give them aid and subsistence here until His Majesty should be pleased to send them an answer to their memorial. In that memorial they asked that His Majesty send troops with them to Ireland to deliver that Kingdom from persecution and tyranny, for all the Irish have raised their hands and wish to see themselves once and for all vassals of the King of Spain. They have represented to His Majesty the facility with which this could be accomplished considering that all the principal persons of the Kingdom have already given their word, that the common people of the Kingdom wish for nothing more than to be free from the yoke of the heretics, that in the kingdom of Scotland they have many kinsmen and friends who would assist them, and they have great hopes of, and correspondence with some catholics in England whose aims are similar. For the execution of these plans, the Earls have begged Your Majesty to be pleased to send them permission to appear in his royal presence and they are still awaiting a reply. This is a summary account of the present position of the Earls.

Memorial of O Neill and O Donnell, undated but forwarded to King Philip III by the Conde de Fuentes with his letter of 13 April 1608.

Description of the lands of the Earls of Tyron and Tyrconel and brief account of their race and their descendence.

The Earls of Tyron and Tyrconel, who were called by the names of Onel and Odonel (until the King of England ordered that those names be not used) have their territories in the north of Ireland, called the province of Ulster (which is one of the largest provinces of that kingdom), and in part of the province of Connaught (which is in the western part of Ireland). The whole province of Ulster is theirs because all the inhabitants are their vassals and have always been so, until this King of England detached many of them for reasons of state and ordered them to cease rendering the vassalage or tribute which they had been accustomed to pay to the Earls and to their ancestors. This province has many very good sea ports which are suitable for all types of ships, more so than any other province of that kingdom, and most of them are in the land of the Earl of Tyrconel. This province is close to Scotland which may be reached in four or five hours of navigation. For this reason the Earls often marry Scottish women and thus it is that they are related to the principal lords of all Scotland, particularly with those of the neighbouring parts, of whom the lord of Ile and Quintir is an uncle of the Earl of Tyrconel and the Earl of Erguil and the lord of Ererton are his cousins; they are among the most powerful lords of that kingdom. The said Earls are lords of the whole province of Ulster and of part of the province of Connaught, in the entrances to which there are very strong passes because of the rivers and bogs by which they are surrounded; consequently their inhabitants are less favoured, therefore stronger, than those of the other provinces and are capable of waging war for the whole kingdom when they join forces and are of one mind.

The Earls are direct descendants of King Gathelo who was married to

Scota, daughter of the Pharao King of Egypt. This Gathelo fled from the plagues with which God punished Egypt through the agency of Moses; he embarked with his people and his wife Scota and did not land until he reached Galicia and, having conquered Biscaya, Asturias and Galicia, he proclaimed himself king of that territory. One of his descendants, a king called Milesius, sent his sons with a fleet of sixty ships, which sailed from the port of La Coruña, to conquer and populate Ireland. This was one thousand years before the birth of Our Lord, according to all the ancient chronicles of Ireland, or seven hundred years, according to other ancient authors who are cited by Pineda[1] in his *Monarquia Eclesiastica*.

Since the time of King Eremon who was the first conqueror of Ireland and son of the said King Milesius until the reign of King Nel, one hundred and fifty kings of that house reigned successively. This King Nel had three sons; the eldest son and heir became king and was called Lagerio; he died without sons and in his reign the catholic faith was received in Ireland, which was about three hundred years after the birth of Christ. The other two sons of King Nel were of the one birth and from them are descended the Earls Onel and Odonel. Because of the rivalry as to which of the two houses would succeed to the kingdom of King Nel, they agreed that each would reign in turn, that is to say that when the heir of Onel was king, on his death the heir of Odonel would succeed to him, and when the latter died, the heir of Onel would reign. After that agreement there were twenty-six kings of those two houses and they were kings of all Ireland. They remained in possession of that kingdom until enmity grew between them and the agreement fell apart. Since then, which is more than seven hundred years ago, there was continuous war between those two houses of Onel and Odonel; the English never found a better opportunity to take possession, as they did, of the kingdom of Ireland. The enmity between the Earls Onel and Odonel lasted until the father of the Earl Odonel (who is here) gave his daughter in marriage to the Earl of Tyron (who also is here). Of this marriage two sons were born; the heir is the Baron of Dungannon who is here with his father; the other is Colonel Don Henrique Onel who is in Your Majesty's service in the States of Flanders. And that marriage caused the unity of those two Earls who joined forces to wage a war of great importance for Christendom, for such was the last war in Ireland.

1. The Franciscan author and historian, Juan de Pineda, a native of Medina del Campo, was born in the early years of the 16th century and died in 1593. The full title of his work mentioned in this document is *La Monarquía Eclesiástica, o Historia Universal del Mundo desde su Creación;* it was published in Salamanca in 1588.

Notes

Page numbers are given at the beginning of each entry.

15 Henry IV of France King Henry's words are recorded by the contemporary English historian, William Camden. They were said in the presence of the Duke of Osuna who repeated them to Camden; quoted by Meehan, *The Fate and Fortunes of O Neill and O Donnell,* p. 125.

26 Conde de Caracena In July of that year, 1602, an English spy reported to Sir George Carew, President of Munster: 'Don Luis de Carillo, Count of Caracena and Governor of the Groyne [Coruña], is the chief favourer of Irish fugitives in Spain. He racks his credit to the utmost to advance their designs.' In 1608, when Caracena had left the governorship of Galicia and had been appointed to Valencia, he wrote to King Philip: 'Señor, distance and change of office are not sufficient to make me forget the great affection I always had for the Catholics of Ireland and now I hear that in La Coruña the Irish miss me . . . I beg Your Majesty to order that the Irish be helped and protected as much as possible and particularly the sons of the catholic nobles who, by order of Your Majesty, are being educated in the College of Santiago.'

38 Frances, daughter of Charles Howard Frances Howard's first husband, Henry Fitzgerald, 12th Earl of Kildare, died in 1597 of wounds received at the Blackwater in July of that year. Her second husband, Henry Brooke, Lord Cobbam, had a position of influence at the English Court in the days of Queen Elizabeth for his father had been the Queen's lord chamberlain and his sister was married to Sir Robert Cecil, afterwards Earl of Salisbury. After the Queen's death, Cobham was implicated in the plot to place Arabella Stuart on the English throne; sentenced to death and reprieved in December 1603, he was taken to the Tower of London from which he was released in 1617, only to die a year later. It was said that Frances abandoned Cobbam after his disgrace and, although very rich, 'would not give him the crumbs that fell from her table.'

39 The Earl of Northampton Henry Howard, Earl of Northampton (1540-1614), had been implicated in the conspiracy with Mary Stuart, for which he suffered a term of imprisonment. In 1600 he was allowed to return to the Court. He was made privy councillor by King James in 1604 and was appointed to the office of privy seal in 1608. Thomas Howard (1561–1626), nephew of Northampton, was made privy councillor on the accession of King James by whom he was created Earl of Suffolk. Charles Howard (1536–1624), lord high admiral, was in command of the English navy against the Spanish Armada of 1588, was joint commander with the Earl of Essex at the sack of Cádiz in 1596 and was created Earl of Nottingham in 1597 by Queen Elizabeth; he was continued in his office of high admiral by King James.

42 **Jacques Francesqui** The Francesqui brothers were catholics of Italian origin, born in Antwerp and reared in England. Jacques Francesqui served with the English army in Ireland and was in Dublin with Sir Christopher Hatton in 1585. He went to Flanders with Colonel Stanley in whose regiment he served first as captain and later as lieutenant-colonel. In July 1602 he is mentioned as an excellent 'enjeneur man' and the 'chiefest' of several experienced officers of the Spanish army of Flanders whom O Neill had asked to be sent out to him in Ireland. After the 'Flight of the Earls', on 7 November 1607, he led a group of officers sent out by the Marqués Spínola, commander-in-chief of the Spanish troops in Flanders, to escort O Neill, O Donnell and their companions on their way from Hal to Brussels where Spinola entertained them to a banquet.

57 **John Bath or Rath** It should be noted that in Spanish documents his name is invariably written with an R: Rath, Rad, Rate, Ratti. O Cianáin, also, spells his name Rath. The fact that it is often written Bath in the English State Papers has led to some confusion between this John Rath and Sir John Bathe of Drumcondra. Both of them were in Spain around the same time and were employed by O Neill on various occasions. Captain Rath's brother, James, was a spy in the pay of the English ambassador at Brussels and the Captain himself eventually offered his services to England. John Bathe of Drumcondra, brother of the famous Jesuit, William Bathe, was a double agent employed by Spain and by England; it was he who killed O Sullivan Bear in Madrid in 1618.

57 **Tadhg O Cianáin** O Cianáin's manuscript, preserved in the archives of the Franciscan monastery at Dún Mhuire, Killiney, was first edited and translated by Fr Paul Walsh in *Archivium Hibernicum*, vols. 2-4, 1913-1915, and was published in book form in 1916 under the title *The Flight of the Earls*. In 1972, *Imeacht na nIarlaí* a modern version of O Cianáin's narrative, was edited by Pádraig de Barra, with an introduction and extensive notes and comments by Cardinal Tomás Ó Fiaich.

65 **Sir George Carew** Sir George Carew was sent as ambassador of James I to France at the end of 1605 and remained in that post until July 1609; not to be confused with his namesake who was president of Munster from January 1600 to May 1603.

66 **Ambrosio Spínola** The Marqués Ambrosio Spínola was a wealthy Italian nobleman of great military talent who had come to the service of

Spain in 1602. He raised an army of 6,000 men at his own expense for the war in Flanders. After his success at the siege of Ostend in 1604, Philip III made him commander-in-chief of the troops in Flanders, secretary of finance and knight of the order of the Golden Fleece.

66 **Spanish Ambassador** Felipe Cardona, Marqués de Guadaleste, was appointed ambassador to Flanders in December 1606. He arrived in Brussels to take up his post in July 1607 and he died in office in that city in August 1616.

66 **Duke of Osuna** The celebrated Don Pedro Tellez Girón, third Duke of Osuna and grandee of Spain, was born at Osuna in southern Spain in 1574. After an early life of dissipation in Seville and in Paris, he served with distinction in the Spanish army of Flanders from 1602 to 1608 when he returned to Spain. Philip III appointed him Viceroy of Sicily in 1611. From 1616 to 1618 he was Viceroy of Naples and had orders from the King for the payment of a pension to Catherine Magennis, Countess of Tyrone, who retired to Naples after her husband's death. Osuna died in Madrid in 1624.

66 **Duke of Aumale** Charles of Lorraine, Duke of Aumale and governor of Picardy, had been one of the leaders of the catholic league in the French wars of religion. He joined the Spanish forces against Henry IV of France and, when the latter converted to catholicism in 1593 and entered Paris, Aumale retreated to Picardy. Driven from Amiens in 1594, he took refuge in Flanders and was granted a pension by the King of Spain. In 1595 he was condemned to death in his absence by the Parliament of Paris. A daughter of his was married to the Marqués Ambrosio Spínola. He died in Brussels in 1631.

73 **Marqués de Aytona** Don Gastón de Moncada, Marqués de Aytona, had been appointed ambassador of Spain in Rome towards the end of 1606. He was to remain in that post until June 1609 when he returned to Spain as Viceroy of Aragón.

73 **Conde de Fuentes** Don Pedro Enríquez de Acevedo, Conde de Fuentes, was governor of the Spanish territory of the Milanese. Born *c.*1530 in Zamora, he was a nephew of the great Duke of Alba under whom he served in Italy in 1557. In 1589 he was named captain-general of Portugal and was successful in defending Lisbon against the expedition of the Prior of Ocrato who was supported by Drake and Norris. He succeeded the Archduke Ernesto as governor of Flanders in February 1595 and took command of the troops in Picardy opposed to Henry IV of France. On his return to Spain in 1596, Philip II named him captain-general of Spain. In 1598 he was made grandee of Spain and member of the Council of State. He was governor and captain-general of the Milanese from 1600 to his death in 1610.

75 **Monsieur de Lorraine** The Duke of Lorraine died on 14 May 1608 but the burial did not take place until 18 July. It was customary in the duchy of Lorraine to follow an elaborate ceremonial on the death of the ruling

duke. The body was embalmed and lay in state for several weeks.

77 **Two Memorials** Translations of these two documents appear in the Appendix, pp. 134-138.

78 **Entretenido** This word is sometimes translated in English as *pensioner* but it may also describe a person in receipt of a retainer fee, or even a salary.

79 **Palazzo Dei Penitenzieri** This Palazzo is now the Hotel Columbus.

99 **Don Diego Brochero** Don Diego Brochero y Anaya, Admiral, Councillor of State, Prior of Hibernia in the order of Malta, had been naval commander of the expedition to Kinsale in 1601. He was appointed Protector of the Irish in Spain in succession to the Conde de Puñonrostro whose death occurred early in 1610.

104 **Monastery of St Dominic** This monastery was destroyed in 1870. It was situated on what is now the Plaza de Santo Domingo, at the left hand corner of the entrance to the Cuesta de Santo Domingo, facing towards the Royal Palace, which is at a distance of about ten minutes' walk. The old palace was destroyed by fire in 1734; the present building was erected in the same place a few years later.

105 **Earl of Birhaven** Donal O Sullivan Beare was granted the title of Conde de Biraven, or Earl of Berehaven, by Philip III in 1617. Philip O Sullivan was not a nephew of the Earl's but a first cousin; the great difference in age between them would have been the cause of Bathe's mistaken assumption. According to Philip's own statements he was 29 years of age in 1618 and Donal was 57. John Bathe was then 48.

106 **Tadeo Huolano** Probably the same as Father Thadaeus Huollanus from Aghadoe, Co. Kerry, whose name appears in the records of the Irish College of Salamanca as having arrived there in July 1603.

108 **Earl of Boduer** The Admiral of Scotland was Sir Francis Stewart, Earl of Bothwell. Both he and his son lived in Flanders and received pensions from the King of Spain.

111 **Hugh Mac Caughwell** The learned and saintly Fr. Mac Caughwell. or Aodh Mac Aingil, became Archbishop of Armagh in April 1626 and died in Rome five months later.

119 **William Trumbull** Sir William Trumbull succeeded to Sir Thomas Edmonds as ambassador of England in Brussels. He retained that post for sixteen years and was recalled in 1625 when Charles I came to the English throne and war broke out between England and Spain.

130 **Shean Crone McDived** Seán Crón Mac Daibhéid of Inishowen left Ireland with the Earls in 1607. In Spain he was referred to as Juan Dabeto, or Daveto.

132 **Burke** Raymond Burke, Baron of Leitrim, was among those who accompanied Red Hugh O Donnell to Spain in January 1602.

132 **Desmond** This was John Fitzgerald, or Don Juan Geraldino, brother of the Súgán Earl of Desmond who died in the Tower of London in 1608.

133 **O Neill's Tombstone** Thanks to the efforts of the late Cardinal Archbishop of Armagh, Tomás Ó Fiaich, the exact location of O Neill's tombstone was identified and the original inscription, as recorded by Father Meehan, has been reproduced.

134 **Memorials** The Spanish originals of these two documents are to be found in *Archivo General de Simancas*, Estado 1297.

Index

Achill, 54

Aghadoe, 142

Aguila, Juan del, 24-29, 135

Ahuinala, *see* Aumale

Aitona, *see* Aytona

Alba, duke of, 141

Albert, Archduke of Austria, governor of Spanish Flanders, 28, 36, 42, 56, 58, 64, 66-69, 71, 73, 77, 81, 91, 92, 94, 108, 113, 118, 122, 136

Alcalá, 133

Alcántara, Order of, 119

Aldobrandini, Cardinal, 28

Amiens, 141

Andermatt, 76

Antwerp, 91, 140

Aranda de Duero, 107

Argyll (Erguil), Earl of, 137

Arias Dávila, Francisco; Conde de Puñonrostro, Councillor of State, Protector of the Irish in Spain, 54, 142

Armada of 1588, 20, 140

Armagh, 23, 60

Armagh, Archbishop of, 93; *see also* Lombard, Peter; MacCaughwell, Hugh; MacGauran, Edmund

Arras, 66

Arundel, Earl of, *see* Howard, Thomas

Asturias, 138

Athenry, 25

Aumale (Ahumala), Duke of, *see* Lorraine, Charles of

Aytona, Marqués de, *see* Moncada, Gastón de

Bagenal, Sir Henry; marshal of the English army in Ireland, 23, 102

Bagenal, Mabel; Countess of Tyrone, 102

Ballindrait, 60

Baltimore, O Driscoll castle of, 28

Bann river, 18, 45

Barberini, Cardinal, 80

Barcelona, 72

Bardec, *see* Mac an Bhaird

Barnardin, Doctor, 129

Basle, 75

Bath, Captain John *see* Rath, John

Bathe (Bateo, Batheo), Francis, 105

Bathe, Sir John, 102-106, 125, 140, 142

Bathe, William, S.J., 102, 140

Bayona (Bayonne), Galicia, 133

Bellinzona, 76

Beltenebros, *see* Cecil, Sir Robert

Benedictine order, 94

Bentivoglio, Guido; Archbishop of Rhodes, Papal Nuncio at Brussels, 66, 71, 73, 76

Berehaven 106

Berehaven (Biraven, Birhaven), Earl of (Conde de), *see* O Sullivan Beare, Donal

Binche, 66, 67

Biscay, 64

Biscaya, *see* Vizcaya

Blacadell, Diego, *see* Blake, James

Blackwater river, 139

Blanco, Pedro, 130, 131

Blount, Charles; Lord Mountjoy, Earl of Devonshire, Viceroy of Ireland, 30, 31, 35, 36, 39, 45, 47, 52, 59

Blount, Christopher; marshall of the English army in Ireland, 33

Blount, Captain James, 20

Boduer (Bothwell), Earl of, *see* Stewart, Francis

Bologna, 71

Bordeaux (Burdeus), 130

Borghese, Cardinal; afterwards Pope Paul V, 71

Borgia, St. Francis, 131

145